HAPPINESS IS JUNK~FREE FOOD

A wide range of dishes to suit all occasions — free from artificial
flavourings, colourings and preservatives.

HAPPINESS IS
JUNK-FREE FOOD

Fight Hyperactivity and Other Food Allergies with Quick and Easy Healthy Meals for All the Family

by

Janet Ash and Dulcie Roberts

Illustrated by Kim Blundell

THORSONS PUBLISHING GROUP
Wellingborough, Northamptonshire

Rochester, Vermont

First published April 1986
Second Impression December 1986
Third Impression April 1987

British Library Cataloguing in Publication Data

Ash, Janet
 Happiness is junk-free food: fight
 hyperactivity and other food allergies with
 quick and easy, healthy meals for all the family.
 1. Cookery (natural foods)
 I Title   II. Roberts, Dulcie
 641.5'637   TX741

 ISBN 0-7225-1231-7

Printed and bound in Great Britain

Happiness is Junk-free Food is a long-needed book to help mothers of problematic children.

The field of nutritional medicine is expanding at a tremendous rate and public demand for this type of medicine is far outstripping the medical profession's willingness to embrace a non-toxic, nutritional approach to the management of illness; instead, it seems to prefer the more toxic drug prescribing approach.

Thus, there is a need for sensible books of this type to help parents care for their children in a way that does not involve drugging or simply ignoring the problem.

This book provides a host of recipes avoiding 'junk' food. Any diet that concentrates on fresh unprocessed foods, de-emphasizing those foods containing chemical additives and refined sugar and flour, is a diet which will inevitably be healthier than the usual British diet.

The authors are to be congratulated on the work that they have put into producing such a useful book.

T. STEPHEN DAVIES M.A., B.Ch.
Medical Advisor to the
Hyperactive Children's Support Group.

ACKNOWLEDGEMENTS

We would like to thank most sincerely all those who have helped us to compile this recipe book.

We have received donations from many manufacturers and we are grateful for their help and support.

Our very special thanks to those who have so generously allowed us to reprint or adapt their recipes. Also, we would like to thank Mrs I. D. Colquhoun and Sally Bunday, Founders of the Hyperactive Children's Support Group, on behalf of all the many families who have been helped by their dedication and devotion. This book has been written on an entirely voluntary basis and proceeds will be donated to the Hyperactive Children's Support Group.

A *Family Cookbook*. Published by the Hyperactive Children's Support Group, Secretary, Sally Bunday, 59 Meadowside, Angmering, Nr. Littlehampton, W. Sussex BN16 4BW.

Mrs Val Kearney, Mrs Jan Wisby, Mr Stewart Rolfe and members of H.A.C.S.G. and other friends too numerous to mention.

Allinsons, Healthways House, West Byfleet, Surrey.

A *Taste of Health* by Sonja Garber. Published by Robert Hale Ltd.

Batchelors Patisserie, 246 Northdown Road, Cliftonville, Thanet, Kent.

Children's Parties by Helen Thomas. Penguin Handbooks.

Eating and Allergy by Robert Eagle. Published by Thorsons.

Farmhouse Fare. Recipes collected by *Farmer's Weekly*. Country Wise Books. Agricultural Press. Hamlyn Publishing Group.

Fast Food, Real Food by Miriam Polunin. Thorsons Publishing Group, Wellingborough, Northamptonshire.

Good Food Gluten Free by Hilda Cherry Hills, c/o Henry Doubleday

Research Association, Convent Lane, Bocking Braintree, Essex. Published by Robert Publications.

Good Housekeeping Wholefood Cookery by Gail Duff. Published by Ebury Press.

Handbook of Nature Cure by T. Glyn Moule, Darrowfield House, St Michaels, St Albans, Herts.

Here's Health Magazine, Newman Turner Publications Ltd, 30 Station Approach, West Byfleet, Surrey.

Jordan's Country Cookbook. Wholewheat Recipes. Holme Mills, Biggleswade.

More for your Money by Shirley Goode and Erica Griffiths. Reprinted by permission of Penguin Books Ltd.

Not Just a Load of Old Lentils by Rose Elliot. Published by Fontana.

Plamil Foods Ltd, Plamil House, Folkestone, Kent.

Soya Foods Ltd, New Maldon House, 1 Blagdon Road, New Maldon, Surrey.

The Alternative Cookbook compiled by Honor J. Campbell. Published by Food Watch, Butts Pond Industrial Estate, Sturminster Newton, Dorset DT10 1AZ.

Random House Inc., New York.

Wholewheat Flour Recipes, St Nicholas Mill, St Nicholas-at-Wade, Thanet, Kent.

To Gill Goldfinch, with grateful thanks for the typing and to Patti Key for her generous help with the proof reading.

Special thanks to Peter, for all his help, and the loan of his cookery books.

Adam, with many thanks for his help.

Very sincere appreciation to Ron, Nigel, the late Mrs Grace Wickham, Friends, Health Food Stores at Dover and Oasis at Canterbury, for their patience, understanding and assistance.

CONTENTS

INTRODUCTION

This recipe book has been especially compiled for hyperactive children and their families and is based on the Feingold Diet.

The exclusion of certain fruits and vegetables which contain salicylates* for four to six weeks presents many problems, and the elimination of all artificial additives, i.e. flavourings, colourings and preservatives, can be both time consuming and frustrating. We have aimed to alleviate these problems so that the entire family can enjoy meals which are wholesome, tasty and safe from artificial additives.

All the recipes are salicylate-free and artificial additive-free. Some are also grain-free, gluten-free, milk-free, and egg-free. Each recipe has been coded so that you may see at a glance if the recipe is suitable for you, to suit your own sensitivity or allergy.

HYPERACTIVE ADULTS can also benefit from the diet.

HELPFUL HINTS

When you start the diet remember to read labels on everything you buy. If ingredients are not listed or if you are unsure about an ingredient then the food is best avoided. Manufacturers are continually changing the ingredients in their products, very often not in our favour. So always be alert.

Keep a guess what? box of allowed treats, permitted fruit, nut bars,

*Salicylates, which are found in certain fruits and vegetables, are naturally occuring substances (closely allied in basic structure to aspirin) to which hyperactive children are sometimes sensitive.

peanuts, etc. Let the child dip into this.

Food and drink. Take some food and drink out with you on short and long trips. Very often a 'whiny' child will be better after a drink and/or snack. This will also stop you from buying the 'wrong' food, and help you stick to the diet. Remember even a mouthful of wrong food can cause a reaction. The H.A.C.S.G. include a safe food list with diet information for members. Tell as many people as possible about the diet. Ask them to keep their eyes open for pure foods. Tell shopkeepers you need foods that do not contain any chemical additives. In this way more pure foods will become available. To improve and maintain optimum health it is better to eat wholefoods rather than refined foods which have had a lot of their goodness removed in processing. By eating foods as near to their natural state as possible, you are also feeding the body with vitamins and minerals in their natural state so that imbalances do not occur. However, we can all benefit from vitamin and mineral supplements from time to time, if these are taken with care.

Eat fresh fruit and vegetables with their skins to provide extra roughage (fibre). Eat more raw foods rather than cooked every day. Start off gradually. Aim to eat some raw fruit at each meal and one salad per day. Avoid all chemical additives in foods. You will be amazed how much better you will feel and look, also how much energy you have. The better our health, the less likely we are to be ill. We also have more resistance to disease, allergies, and pollutants in the atmosphere.

Baking Powder
To make your own use one part bicarbonate of soda (baking soda) to two parts cream of tartar.

Bicarbonate of Soda (Baking soda)
This is said to destroy vitamin B_1, riboflavin, pyridoxine (vitamin B_6) and vitamin C. Therefore do not use in excess.

Flours: 81 per cent, 85 per cent
These are kinder to children's digestive systems in a gradual progression to wholemeal, and are well accepted by people who do not like 'brown' cooking.

Brown Rice Flour
If you find difficulty in obtaining brown rice flour, health food stores should stock this. Alternatively grind whole brown rice in a grain mill. This method is cheaper.

Arrowroot, Tapioca and Sago
These are recommended for people suffering from food allergies, but have little nutritional value. Millet (obtainable whole, flaked or as a flour) is better.

Uncooked Egg White
Destroys biotin, one of the B vitamins. Avidin in the white latches on to biotin, making it unavailable to the body.

Sulphur Dioxide
Wash dried fruits well in boiling water to remove most of the sulphur dioxide. Rinse well in cold water. Boiling should then remove any residue.

Lemon, Pineapple or Grapefruit Juice
Use any of these juices to preserve the colour of cut pieces of fruit e.g. pear or banana.

Permitted Stewed Fruit Juices
Strain any extra juice and use as a drink, or mix with other permitted fruit juices. Call drinks 'fruit cocktails'. Add a slice of lemon and ice cubes for extra interest.

To Wean Off Tea and Coffee
Make permitted drinks in a small teapot. It will be fun for the child to pour out his/her own 'special drink'.

Cocoa
Even pure additive-free cocoa contains caffeine — a stimulant. Use carob as a chocolate substitute.

Goat's Milk
Keeps four days in a fridge, freezes well and will keep for two months in a freezer.

Plain Natural Yogurt
Can be used in place of sour cream.

Scrambled Eggs or Pancakes
Make with water instead of milk.

Cauliflower or Courgettes (Zucchini)
Cook with a bay leaf.

Jerusalem Artichokes
Serve as an extra vegetable with any meal. Trim, scrub skins and steam, boil or bake.

Garlic
Is a good cleanser for the body. Eat parsley to help get rid of 'garlic breath'.

Ground Mustard Seed
Can be obtained from health food stores.

Oils Recommended
The best oils to use for salad dressings are safflower or sunflower oils which are high in essential fatty acids. Try to use cold-pressed oils as these have not gone through a heat treated process using various chemicals to bleach and deodorize them, although expensive, unrefined oils are much healthier. Eicosapentaenoic (EPA) is another essential fatty acid found in oils, coming from fatty fish such as herrings, mackerel, sprats, salmon and sardines.

There is a school of thought which says it is not good to use highly polyunsaturated oils such as safflower or sunflower for frying as they can cause dangerous particles called free radicals to be released, which may accelerate the ageing process, particularly if there is no vitamin E present. Probably the best oils to use for cooking are olive or sesame, or a little butter, occasionally. If you use other oils, make sure they have vitamin E added; this also applies to margarines.

Baking with Oils
When converting from a recipe using margarine, reduce the fat

content by one third i.e. 6 oz (170g, ⅔ cup) margarine = 4 fl oz (125ml, ½ cup) oil. Oil is not suitable for use where a solid fat is melted and used as a binding agent e.g. flapjacks. (Reproduced by kind permission of Foodwatch.)

Frying
Keep to a minimum — grill instead.

Pork
Is suspect.

Malt
Is suspect. So look out for malt and malt flavouring, especially in breakfast cereals if these upset the child.

Sugar
Keep all sugar to a minimum (see page 18).

Vanilla Flavoured Sugar
Put a vanilla pod (bean) in a jar of raw cane sugar.

Castor/Icing Sugar Substitute
Grind raw cane Demerara sugar.

Lumpy Moist Sugar
Put in a basin and cover with a damp cloth, or put in a polythene bag and crush with a rolling pin.

Dill and Fennel (Herbs)
Have a sweet flavour. Will help to cut down the amount of sugar used. Obtainable at health food stores.

Sweet Cicely (Herb)
Is a very good sugar saver. Not very easily obtained, but very easy to grow.

To Toast Nuts
Spread out on a baking sheet and put in a moderate oven for approx. ten minutes.

Hazelnuts
Not usually necessary to skin, but if desired, prepare as for toasted nuts and keep in oven for approx. 20 minutes. Rub off skins with a clean tea towel or kitchen paper.

Freezing
If you own a freezer you will not miss convenience foods so much if you:
1. Make large batches of burgers, rissoles, fish, cakes, stews, soups, main meals, etc.
2. Cook double quantities of pulses and whole brown rice. Freeze in small amounts. You will soon have a variety which you can use in salads and stews, etc. Will also keep several days in a 'fridge.

Pulses
It is better to use whole beans than split.

Pot Barley
Use the whole (pot) barley in place of pearl barley.

Pressure Cooker
Is a marvellous cooking aid especially for pulses which take from 10-30 minutes depending on variety, or whole brown rice which takes approx. 15 minutes.

Food Flask
Useful for 'any time meals', packed lunches, travelling or even at home.

Salad Spinner
A must — spins washed salads dry in seconds.

Yogurt and Cheese Maker
Very useful. Deva Bridge make a yogurt and cheese maker which do not use electricity. See list of suppliers on page 257.

Recipe Books
To keep clean when in use, place open book in a clear polythene (plastic) bag.

DO'S AND DONT'S

DO try and buy fresh vegetables, organically grown if possible, and which have not been on display outside shops where they can collect lead and fumes from petrol.

DO try and steam vegetables, cook using a simple steaming basket. The flavour is much better and the vitamins are not so easily lost.

DO use the water you have cooked vegetables in for gravies, soups, stews, etc. It contains a lot of nutrients.

DO cook vegetables without salt. They have salt naturally occurring in them.

DO use sea salt or salt substitute where seasoning is essential. Free flowing salt has been chemically treated.

DO read labels and see how many times salt and sugar are added to processed food.

DO buy free range eggs. The taste and texture, even the smell, are completely different.

DO use bought frozen food sparingly even if considered safe. Most frozen vegetables are treated with a chemical to help preserve colour.

DO freeze your own meats and vegetables.

DO make and freeze your own complete meals.

DO eat cooked leftover vegetables in salads or mashed in sandwiches. Avoid reheating.

DO remember to wash all fruit and vegetables before use, and to eat their skins. Peel only when tough or bitter. Vitamins, minerals and flavours are concentrated just under the skins. They also add natural fibre to the diet.

DO scrub skins of citrus fruit. These may have been dyed.

DO remember to wean your child off tea and coffee. These are stimulants. See drink section on page 216 and hints on page 11.

DO use plain white kitchen paper towels. Dyes from coloured kitchen paper can come off on to food.

DO try and use stainless steel saucepans instead of aluminium ones.

DO keep persevering with the diet. Even a small amount of 'wrong' food will cause a reaction.

DO NOT overcook food, especially vegetables as all the vitamins will be lost into the water.

DO NOT cook green potatoes. They contain a poisonous alkaloid,

solanin. Also avoid potatoes with blight.
DO NOT buy fruit drinks. These are not pure fruit juices.
DO NOT buy dented cans, as lead could leak from a broken seal.
DO NOT store food or drink in their cans as lead from the solder may be absorbed into the food.

Sugar

Sugar consumption is generally too high for our own good. Reports suggest that over 100lb (approx. 45 kg) per person per year is eaten. Most processed foods (even savoury and vegetable foods) have sugar and salt added to them and both are very often added in cooking and again in serving. As sugar may well be one of the causes of hyperactivity and other diseases, one of the first aims should be to cut down all added sugar in any form.

A lot of mothers report further improvement in their children after removal of sugar from their diet, so this is well worth trying gradually. Greater consumption of sugar (whether white or brown) spells inferior nutrition, because sugar provides empty calories that have been stripped of minerals and vitamins.

Those suffering from hypoglycaemia (low blood sugar) do not need extra sugar. Common symptoms of this are dizziness, headaches, irritability or increased hyperactivity before meals. Mood swings are also noticeable.

Sugar occurs naturally in fruits and some vegetables. When sweetening is required use natural raw cane sugars and pure honey to the minimum. Honey is absorbed slowly in the body and keeps our body energy stable. White sugar or 'coloured brown' sugar send us on highs and lows of energy and have no nutritional value.

You may find some of our recipes are not sweet enough for you yet!!! Gradually reduce the amount of sugar you use. After a while it will become quite natural to use smaller quantities.

N.B. Golden Syrup is a derivative of white sugar. Use honey instead.

Seasonings

It is better for small children not to have highly spiced foods and it is a good idea to cut down on salt and pepper. Flavour foods with herbs which are tasty and beneficial.

While a little salt is very necessary to us, too much is not and can be very harmful. All processed foods seem to have salt and sugar added to them. Salt occurs naturally in vegetables and need not be added in cooking. If you need to use salt, sea salt or rock salt are best as these have formed naturally. They contain essential trace elements lacking in refined free running salt which has usually had chemicals added to it.

It is a good idea to use black pepper (peppercorns) in place of ground pepper for the same reasons. Salt and pepper mills are easily available.

Natural Food Flavours
Use juice, peel or pulp of the selected fruit/s.

Natural Food Colours

Yellow
Lemon rind
Saffron
Annatto
Turmeric
Onion skins

Green
Any edible green leaf

Blue
Red cabbage

Pink/Red
Beetroot (beet) juice: Use 1 to 2 teaspoons bottled juice, or sieve some cooked beetroot (beet) and use strained juice. Hibiscus herb tea: pour a little boiling water over a hibiscus tea bag. Leave to stand for 10 minutes. Use until desired colour is reached. Natural food colours are available from Foodwatch (page 256).

BREAKFASTS

HONEY CINNAMON GRAPEFRUIT

Grain Free	Gluten Free	Milk Free	Egg Free

Imperial (Metric)

1-2 *teaspoons honey*
½ *teaspoon cinnamon*
2 *grapefruit, peeled and segmented*

American

1-2 *teaspoons honey*
½ *teaspoon cinnamon*
2 *grapefruit, peeled and segmented*

1. Heat the honey with the cinnamon until almost boiling, then pour over the cold grapefruit segments.

Note: Serve with chopped walnuts (English walnuts) or hazelnuts.

GRAPEFRUIT AND MELON REFRESHER

Grain Free	Gluten Free	Milk Free	Egg Free

This is really good to start the day with, as there's lots of vitamin C in this recipe. Alternatively use it as a sweet.

Imperial (Metric)

1 small melon
1 grapefruit, peeled
Juice of ½ lime
1-2 tablespoons clear honey or to taste

American

1 small melon
1 grapefruit, peeled
Juice of ½ lime
1-2 tablespoons clear honey or to taste

1. Cut the melon and grapefruit into cubes.

2. Add the juice and honey and mix well. Serve topped with chopped hazelnuts, walnuts (English walnuts), desiccated coconut, or dates.

ALPINE BREAKFAST

Serves 2

Egg Free

Imperial (Metric)

1 grapefruit, peeled and segmented
1 pear, peeled and chopped
1 oz (30g) chopped dates or figs
1 oz (30g) nuts of choice (brazil, hazelnuts, walnuts or grated coconut)
1 oz (30g) porridge oats or wheatgerm
1 teaspoon honey
¼ pint (140ml) low fat natural yogurt

American

1 grapefruit, peeled and segmented
1 pear, peeled and chopped
2 tablespoons chopped dates or figs
3 tablespoons nuts of choice (brazil, hazelnuts, English walnuts or grated coconut)
¼ cup rolled oats or wheatgerm
1 teaspoon honey
⅔ cup plain yogurt

1. Chop the grapefruit and place in a bowl.

2. Add the chopped pear to prevent it discolouring.

3. Mix the rest of the ingredients with the fruit.

4. If possible, leave in the refrigerator or a cool place for an hour before serving, or keep overnight in the refrigerator so that it will be ready for breakfast.

CRUNCHY MUESLI

Milk Free   Egg Free

You can buy your muesli base from health shops, or mix your own if you wish. This is usually made up of oats, wheat flakes, rye flakes or wheatgerm.

Imperial (Metric)	*American*
4 tablespoons safflower or sunflower oil	4 tablespoons safflower or sunflower oil
3 tablespoons honey	3 tablespoons honey
1 teaspoon natural vanilla essence (optional)	1 teaspoon natural vanilla essence (optional)
1 lb (455g) muesli base	2 cups muesli base
2 oz (55g) sesame seeds	½ cup sesame seeds
2 oz (55g) sunflower seeds	½ cup sunflower seeds
2 oz (55g) hazelnuts, walnuts or brazil nuts, chopped	½ cup hazelnuts, English walnuts or brazil nuts, chopped

1. Heat the oil and honey. Add the vanilla essence, muesli base, seeds and nuts.

2. Remove from the heat and stir well to coat. Spread the mixture on to a baking tray and bake in oven at 375°F/190°C (Gas Mark 5) for 30 minutes. You have to stir it quite often to stop it burning on top.

3. Store in a covered jar. Serve with milk, yogurt, fresh or dried fruits.

CINNAMON TOAST

Egg Free

Imperial (Metric)	American
2-3 slices wholemeal bread	2-3 slices wholewheat bread
unsalted butter or margarine	unsalted butter or margarine
½ teaspoon ground cinnamon	½ teaspoon ground cinnamon
2 teaspoons ground demerara or soft brown muscovado sugar	2 teaspoons ground demerara or soft brown muscovado sugar

1. Toast the bread. Butter it.

2. Mix the cinnamon and sugar and sprinkle on top of the toast.

3. Grill for a minute or two until the sugar melts. Serve hot.

FRENCH TOAST

Imperial (Metric)	American
1 free range egg	1 free range egg
1 tablespoon milk	1 tablespoon milk
sea salt and freshly ground pepper to taste	sea salt and freshly ground pepper to taste
2 slices wholemeal bread	2 slices wholewheat bread
safflower or sunflower oil	safflower or sunflower oil

1. Beat the egg and milk together and season.

2. Dip the bread into the egg mixture, then fry in hot oil for a minute on each side until browned.

FRUITY BREAKFAST YOGURT

Grain Free   Gluten Free   Egg Free

Imperial (Metric)

2 grapefruit, peeled and segmented
2 bananas, sliced
½ small melon, cubed
6-8 dates, chopped
¾ pint (425ml) natural yogurt

American

2 grapefruit, segmented
2 bananas, sliced
½ small melon, cubed
6-8 dates, chopped
2 cups plain yogurt

Stir the fruit into the yogurt. Chill and serve with wholemeal (wholewheat) toast, or Cinnamon and Walnut Drop Scones (Pancakes) (see page 29).

YOGURT

Grain Free   Gluten Free   Egg Free

Try making your own, it's much cheaper, and easy once you get the hang of it. It is a wonderful health giving food.

1. Heat 1 pint (570ml/2½ cups) milk almost to the boil.

2. Allow to cool until you can keep your little finger in the milk for 10 seconds, comfortably.

3. Mix 2 tablespoons natural (plain) yogurt with a little of the milk to make a smooth mixture, then combine with the rest.

4. Leave covered with a tea cloth or in a jar with a loosely fitting cap, in a warm kitchen, airing cupboard or, in winter, on the mantlepiece over the fire. You need to provide a steady warmth.

5. Check in 3 to 8 hours to see if it has set. Then put in the refrigerator.

Alternatively, sterilize a flask by pouring boiling water into it and leaving for 5 minutes. A wide necked flask is easier to spoon the yogurt out of when set. Do not fill the flask completely to the top, as you must leave room for the gases inside to expand. Pour in the mixture, screw down and leave to set, usually for about 6 hours. For a thick set yogurt, stir a tablespoon of dried skimmed milk into the yogurt starter before adding the milk. To serve you can just stir in some honey, and top with chopped walnuts (English walnuts) or hazelnuts, and fresh or soft dried dates. Add your own permitted fruit such as pineapple, mashed banana, chopped, puréed or liquidized figs.

Caution: Bananas may cause reaction in somebody who is highly sensitive to salicylates.

SOYA (SOY) YOGURT

Grain Free	Gluten Free	Milk Free	Egg Free

To make yogurt from soya (soy) milk, you just follow the same procedure but only heat the milk until it rises in the pan, stirring all the time. To make a thicker yogurt, use some concentrated soya (soy) milk with the ordinary soya (soy) milk.
Use a vegetarian starter available from most health shops.

TO MAKE YOUR CURD CHEESE

Grain Free	Gluten Free	Egg Free

Add ½ teaspoon salt to 1 pint (570ml/2½ cups) of the homemade yogurt. Pour into a piece of muslin and hang it overnight to drain. Add your own chopped chives, a little garlic or sage.

Note: The *Deva Bridge* Yogurt and Cheese Maker is very useful. (See list of suppliers on page 257.)

OATMEAL PORRIDGE

Milk Free	Egg Free

Imperial (Metric)	*American*
1½ pints (850ml) water	3¾ cups water
¼ level teaspoon ground sea salt	¼ level teaspoon ground sea salt
4 oz (115g) medium oatmeal	1 cup oatmeal

1. Bring the water to the boil, add the salt, then gradually stir in the oatmeal.

2. Cover pan and simmer for 20 minutes. When cooked, add cinnamon or fresh fruit for extra flavour. Serve with milk, soya (soy) milk, or yogurt and raw cane sugar or honey. Makes a warming breakfast on a cold day.

WHOLE MILLET PORRIDGE

Gluten Free   Egg Free

Imperial (Metric)

4 oz (115g) whole millet
1 pint (570ml) boiling water
½ teaspoon sea salt

American

½ cup whole millet
2½ cups boiling water
½ teaspoon sea salt

1. Cook together gently for 25-30 minutes, when millet should be soft and fluffy. Serve with milk or yogurt, honey and allowed fruit of choice.

MILLET FLAKES

Gluten Free   Egg Free

Use 2 tablespoons per person. Soak overnight in fruit juice or fruit juice and water. Heat slowly until it thickens. Add cinnamon for extra flavour. Serve as above.

CINNAMON AND WALNUT DROP SCONES (PANCAKES)

Makes 12

Imperial (Metric)	American
4 oz (115g) 100% wholemeal flour	1 cup wholewheat flour
1½ teaspoons baking powder	1½ teaspoons baking powder
¼ teaspoon sea salt	¼ teaspoon sea salt
½ teaspoon cinnamon	½ teaspoon cinnamon
1 tablespoon raw cane sugar	1 tablespoon raw cane sugar
2 tablespoons safflower or sunflower oil	2 tablespoons safflower or sunflower oil
1 free range egg	1 free range egg
¼ pint (140ml) milk	⅔ cup milk
2 oz (55g) walnuts, chopped finely	½ cup English walnuts, chopped finely

1. Sift together the flour, baking powder, sea salt, cinnamon and sugar.

2. Make a well in the centre and add the oil and egg, then gradually add the milk and walnuts (English walnuts).

3. Lightly oil a frying pan or griddle (skillet).

4. Drop tablespoons of the mixture on to the griddle and cook for a minute or two until bubbles appear on the top. Turn over and cook the other side until golden brown.

5. Serve with butter or low fat cottage cheese.

PARSNIP OR SWEDE (RUTABAGA) FRITTERS

Egg Free

These are good for breakfast on a cold morning if you have the vegetables left over from the night before.

Imperial (Metric)

1-2 large parsnips or ½ swede (medium sized)

½ oz (15g) unsalted butter or margarine

2 oz (55g) 81%-85% wheatmeal flour

sea salt and freshly ground pepper

2 tablespoons safflower or sunflower oil

American

1-2 large parsnips or ½ medium sized rutabaga

1¼ tablespoons unsalted butter or margarine

½ cup 81%-85% wheatmeal flour

sea salt and freshly ground pepper

2 tablespoons safflower or sunflower oil

1. Boil the vegetable, then mash well.

2. Rub the fat into the flour and add to the parsnips or swede (rutabaga), with salt and pepper to taste. Mix well.

3. Heat the oil in a pan and drop spoonsful of the mixture into it, and fry until golden brown.

Note: Serve with scrambled, poached or fried eggs and wholemeal (wholewheat) toast.

SALMON KEDGEREE

Gluten Free   Milk Free

Tuna fish may be used as an alternative to salmon. It is easiest if you've already cooked the rice the night before. Also good as a main meal.

Imperial (Metric)	*American*
6 oz (170g) brown rice	1 cup brown rice
1 large tin salmon	1 large can salmon
2 tablespoons chopped parsley	2 tablespoons chopped parsley
3 hard boiled eggs	3 hard boiled eggs
sea salt and freshly ground pepper to taste if necessary	sea salt and freshly ground pepper to taste if necessary
a little safflower or sunflower oil	a little safflower or sunflower oil

1. Mix the rice with the salmon, parsley and two of the hard boiled eggs, chopped. Season if necessary.

2. Heat a little oil in a pan, then add the mixture and heat through.

3. Put on to a warmed serving dish, and arrange the other egg, sliced, on top.

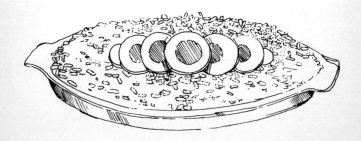

HERRINGS IN OATMEAL

Egg Free

Imperial (Metric)	**American**
4 herrings	4 herrings
sea salt and freshly ground pepper	sea salt and freshly ground pepper
oatmeal	oatmeal
a little milk	a little milk
safflower or sunflower oil	safflower or sunflower oil
lemon and parsley for garnish	lemon and parsley for garnish

1. Have the herrings boned, and the heads removed.

2. Add salt and pepper to taste to the oatmeal. Dip the herrings in the milk, then in the oatmeal.

3. Only use a little oil to cook the herrings, as they contain a lot of oil themselves. Cook on both sides until browned.

4. Drain on plain white kitchen paper towels and serve with lemon, parsley and oatcakes (see page 33).

Note: Can also be served as a main meal.

OATCAKES

Makes about 12

Egg Free

Imperial (Metric)	*American*
6 oz (170g) medium oatmeal	1½ cups medium oatmeal
2 oz (55g) wholemeal flour	½ cup wholewheat flour
1 teaspoon baking powder	1 teaspoon baking powder
½ teaspoon sea salt	½ teaspoon sea salt
3 oz (85g) vegetable margarine	⅓ cup vegetable margarine
3 tablespoons water	3 tablespoons water
sunflower or sesame seeds	sunflower or sesame seeds

1. Combine the oatmeal, wholemeal (wholewheat) flour, baking powder and salt.

2. Put the margarine and water in a saucepan and bring to the boil.

3. Pour on to the dry ingredients and mix to a soft dough, adding more boiling water if necessary.

4. Roll out thinly on a board dusted with oatmeal. Sprinkle with sesame or sunflower seeds and press well down on to the dough with the rolling pin.

5. Cut into triangles and bake for 20 minutes at 350°F/180°C (Gas Mark 4), or cook on a moderately hot griddle (skillet), until oatcakes start to curl at the edges.

DRIED FRUIT SHAKE

Egg Free

Imperial (Metric)	American
5 oz (140g) cooked dried pears	1 cup cooked dried pears
1 pint (570ml) low fat natural yogurt (cow's, or goat's)	2½ cups plain yogurt (cow's, or goat's)
2 teaspoons thin honey	2 teaspoons thin honey
1 tablespoon wheatgerm	1 tablespoon wheatgerm

1. Put all the ingredients in a liquidizer and blend until smooth. This is a wonderfully nourishing drink.

BANANA AND LEMON HEALTH DRINK

Makes 2 small glasses

Grain Free   Gluten Free   Egg Free

Imperial (Metric)	American
¼ pint (140ml) natural yogurt	⅔ cup plain yogurt
1 large banana	1 large banana
2 teaspoons lemon juice	2 teaspoons lemon juice
2 teaspoons honey	2 teaspoons honey

1. Liquidize all the ingredients together until frothy. Serve with slices of wholemeal (wholewheat) toast and you have an instant nourishing breakfast.

Note: Bananas may cause reactions.

HAZELNUT MILK SHAKE

Grain Free   Gluten Free   Egg Free

Imperial (Metric)

½ *pint (285ml) milk (cow's, goat's or*
  soya)
2 *oz (55g) hazelnuts, finely ground*
2 *teaspoons honey*
1 *fresh pear*

American

1⅓ *cups milk (cow's, goat's or soy)*
½ *cup hazelnuts, finely ground*
2 *teaspoons honey*
1 *fresh pear*

1. Liquidize all the ingredients together until smooth. This
   makes a delicious protein packed drink.

Note: For a milk free recipe use soya (soy) milk.

DELICIOUS SEED MILK

Grain Free   Gluten Free   Milk Free   Egg Free

A nourishing breakfast is very important for all children. This
drink is highly nutritious and digestible.

Imperial (Metric)

1 *oz (30g) sunflower seeds*
1 *oz (30g) sesame seeds, preferably*
  toasted
½ *pint (285ml) water*
¼ *pint (140ml) pineapple or pear*
  juice
4-5 *dried figs or 6 dried dates (these*
  may be better soaked)

American

¼ *cup sunflower seeds*
¼ *cup sesame seeds, preferably*
  toasted
1⅓ *cups water*
⅔ *cup pineapple or pear juice*
4-5 *dried figs or 6 dried dates (these*
  may be better soaked)

1. Grind the seeds, then liquidize together with the remaining
   ingredients.

CASHEW NUT MILK

Grain Free   Gluten Free   Milk Free   Egg Free

Imperial (Metric)

4 oz (115g) cashew nuts
½ pint (285ml) water or more

American

¾ cup cashew nuts
1⅓ cups water or more

1. Grind the dry cashew nuts well.

2. Slowly add the water to form a paste, then more to make a milk.

3. You can add a little honey if you wish.

4. Use with cereals, or liquidize with a banana, or dates, or other allowed fruits to make a nut milk shake.

Note: Bananas may cause reactions.

2.

SOUPS

These really are easy to make, and are cheap, nourishing and tasty, particularly on a cold winter's day, served with chunks of bread, grated cheese and salad. The secret is to make a good stock. For vegetable stock just save the liquor strained from cooked vegetables. For a chicken or meat stock, put the chicken carcass, meat bones or trimmings into a large saucepan. Add an onion, carrot, 1-2 celery stalks and tops, sprigs of parsley and a bay leaf. Cover with cold water, then bring to the boil and simmer (not boil or it will go cloudy), for 3-4 hours. Strain and keep in the refrigerator. This must be boiled up every two to three days, or frozen.

EVERYTHING SOUP

Grain Free	Gluten Free	Milk Free	Egg Free

Imperial (Metric)

1 onion
1 clove of garlic (optional)
outside leaves of green vegetables
tops of leeks
outside stalk and leaves of celery
carrots
a potato etc. until you have 1 lb
   (455g) vegetables
2 teaspoons mixed herbs
1 pint (570ml) vegetable stock or
   water
sea salt and freshly ground pepper to
   taste

American

1 onion
1 clove of garlic (optional)
outside leaves of green vegetables
tops of leeks
outside stalk and leaves of celery
carrots
a potato etc. until you have 1 pound
   vegetables
2 teaspoons mixed herbs
2½ cups vegetable stock or water
sea salt and freshly ground pepper to
   taste

1. Lightly oil a frying pan (skillet) and gently sauté chopped onion, and garlic if used, until soft.

2. Add rest of vegetables, herbs and stock or water to barely cover.

3. Simmer until cooked (about 20-30 minutes).

4. Put through blender, and season to taste. Reheat and enjoy. It's never the same twice! Will freeze.

CAULIFLOWER SOUP

Grain Free   Gluten Free   Egg Free

Imperial (Metric)

1 medium sized cauliflower
1 small onion
1 tablespoon chopped parsley
1 bay leaf
1 pint (570ml) stock plus ½ pint
   (285ml) milk [or 1½ pints
   (850ml) stock]
sea salt and freshly ground pepper to
   taste
squeeze of lemon juice

American

1 medium sized cauliflower
1 small onion
1 tablespoon chopped parsley
1 bay leaf
2½ cups stock plus 1⅓ cups milk (or
   3¾ cups stock)
sea salt and freshly ground pepper to
   taste
squeeze of lemon juice

1. Divide the cauliflower into florets and put into a large saucepan with the onion, parsley, bay leaf, stock, milk and seasoning. Cook gently for 30 minutes.

2. Remove the bay leaf, then liquidize. Squeeze a little lemon juice into the soup, and season again if necessary to taste. Will freeze.

MINESTRONE

Gluten Free   Milk Free   Egg Free

Imperial (Metric)

about 1 lb (455g) mixed vegetables (onions, courgettes, runner beans, leeks, turnips, celery or carrots)
2 tablespoons safflower or sunflower oil
1 clove garlic
4 oz (115g) cooked kidney beans
2 oz (55g) long grain brown rice
1½ pints (850ml) water or vegetable stock
pinch sage, oregano and marjoram
sea salt and freshly ground pepper

American

about 1 pound mixed vegetables (onions, zucchini, runner beans, leeks, turnips, celery or carrots)
2 tablespoons safflower or sunflower oil
1 clove garlic
⅔ cup cooked kidney beans
⅓ cup long grain brown rice
3¾ cups water or vegetable stock
pinch sage, oregano and marjoram
sea salt and freshly ground pepper

1. Prepare the vegetables and chop into small pieces.

2. Sauté them in the oil with the crushed garlic for 10 minutes.

3. Add the beans, rice, water or stock, herbs and seasoning.

4. Bring to the boil and simmer for 30 minutes. Will freeze.

BORTSCH

Imperial (Metric)	*American*
1 lb (455g) raw beetroot	1 pound raw beets
1¾ pints (1 litre) stock	4½ cups stock
4 oz (115g) carrots	⅔ cup carrots
4 oz (115g) cabbage	1 cup cabbage
4 oz (115g) celery	1 cup celery
1 bay leaf	1 bay leaf
1 tablespoon chopped parsley	1 tablespoon chopped parsley
pinch cumin	pinch cumin
pinch thyme	pinch thyme
sea salt and freshly ground pepper to taste	sea salt and freshly ground pepper to taste
grated rind and juice of 1 lemon	grated rind and juice of 1 lemon
2 tablespoons sour cream or yogurt	2 tablespoons sour cream or yogurt

1. Peel and slice the beetroot (beet) thinly and simmer in the stock for about 15 minutes.

2. Prepare and chop the other vegetables and add to the beetroot (beet) with the herbs and spices, seasoning and lemon rind and juice.

3. Simmer for about 30 minutes or until the vegetables are soft, then discard the bay leaf. Will freeze if desired.

4. Just before serving stir in 2 tablespoons of sour cream or yogurt.

CARROT AND LEMON SOUP

Grain Free   Gluten Free   Milk Free   Egg Free

Imperial (Metric)

1 onion
2 sticks celery
6 medium sized carrots
1 tablespoon safflower or sunflower
   oil
grated rind and juice of ½ lemon
1 bay leaf
1½ pints (850ml) stock or water
sea salt and freshly ground pepper to
   taste
chopped parsley to serve

American

1 onion
2 stalks celery
6 medium sized carrots
1 tablespoon safflower or sunflower
   oil
grated rind and juice of ½ lemon
1 bay leaf
3¾ cups stock or water
sea salt and freshly ground pepper to
   taste
chopped parsley to serve

1. Chop onion, celery and carrots finely and sauté gently in oil until the vegetables begin to soften, about 5-10 minutes.

2. Add half of the grated lemon rind, the bay leaf and stock or water, and simmer for about 45 minutes.

3. Liquidize, then add the rest of the lemon rind, and the lemon juice and seasoning to taste.

4. Serve sprinkled with chopped parsley or fresh thyme or marjoram when available. Will freeze.

WATERCRESS SOUP

| Grain Free | Gluten Free | Milk Free | Egg Free |

This is also delicious served cold on a hot summer's day. Chill well before serving.

Imperial (Metric)

1 *large potato*
1 *medium turnip*
1 *onion*
1 *tablespoon chopped parsley*
1 *bunch of watercress*
1 *tablespoon safflower or sunflower*
  oil
1 *pint (570ml) vegetable stock*
sea salt and freshly ground pepper

American

1 *large potato*
1 *medium turnip*
1 *onion*
1 *tablespoon chopped parsley*
1 *bunch of watercress*
1 *tablespoon safflower or sunflower*
  oil
2½ *cups vegetable stock*
sea salt and freshly ground pepper

1. Peel the potato, turnip and onion, and chop finely. Wash the parsley and watercress, saving two or three sprigs of watercress to garnish, then chop finely.

2. Sauté the onion, turnip and potato in the oil for a minute or two. Add the chopped watercress and parsley and stock. Season and simmer gently for 15 minutes until the vegetables are tender.

3. Liquidize, and add the remaining watercress leaves to garnish.

LEEK AND POTATO SOUP

Grain Free	Gluten Free	Milk Free	Egg Free

Imperial (Metric)

1 tablespoon safflower oil
2 lb (900g) leeks, trimmed, sliced and washed
1 medium onion, skinned and chopped
1 lb (455g) potatoes, peeled and sliced
2 pints (1.15 litres) vegetable stock
sea salt and freshly ground pepper to taste
chopped chives to garnish

American

1 tablespoon safflower oil
2 pounds leeks, trimmed, sliced and washed
1 medium onion, skinned and chopped
1 pound potatoes, peeled and sliced
5 cups vegetable stock
sea salt and freshly ground pepper to taste
chopped chives to garnish

1. Heat the oil in a large saucepan and sauté the vegetables for 5 minutes.

2. Add the stock and seasoning and bring to the boil. Cover and simmer for about 45 minutes until the vegetables are tender.

3. Cool the soup, then liquidize, or rub through a sieve. Reheat, sprinkle with chopped chives to garnish, and serve with chunks of wholemeal (wholewheat) bread.

3.

MAIN MEALS

FISH

Fish make the quickest and most nourishing meals. White fish can be grilled on an oiled grill pan for 2-3 minutes on each side, or baked in the oven for 15-20 minutes. You can add more flavours by sprinkling the fish with sesame seeds, mixed herbs, soya/tamari sauce, lemon juice, or chopped fennel. Just brush the fish with a little oil or lemon juice first to help the flavourings to stick.

Mackerel can be baked or grilled, it can be stuffed, or cooked with onion rings. Trout can be flavoured from the inside with herbs such as fennel.

Finnan haddock, if you can find it, has no artificial colour added. To cook, simply poach it by putting it in a large saucepan and covering for 4 minutes with boiling water or sauté in a little butter until cooked. Makes delicious kedgeree or pâté.

FISH FINGERS (FISH STICKS)

Milk Free

1. Use fairly thick coley fillets, as cod tends to disintegrate. Chill the fish thoroughly, as it is then easier to handle.

2. Cut into straight fingers, trimming the ends square. Dip into wholemeal (wholewheat) flour, then beaten egg and brown breadcrumbs.

3. Leave in the refrigerator for the coating to harden, for at least an hour.

4. Fry in oil. Will freeze.

Note: If coley is unavailable, use other firm white fish.

ROLL MOP HERRINGS

Grain Free	Gluten Free	Milk Free	Egg Free

Imperial (Metric)	American
4 herrings	4 herrings
4 tablespoons white vinegar	4 large tablespoons white vinegar
¼ pint (140ml) water	⅔ cup water
bay leaf	bay leaf
6 peppercorns	6 peppercorns
1 large onion cut into rings	1 large onion cut into rings

1. Clean, bone and fillet the fish or ask your fishmonger to do it. Wash them well.

2. Roll them up starting from the tail end and pack them closely together in a baking dish.

3. Mix the vinegar and water, pour it over the fish, then add the bay leaf, peppercorns, and onion rings.

4. Bake in the oven, in a covered dish, 350°F/180°C (Gas Mark 4) for 40 minutes. Serve cold with salad.

BAKED FISH IN YOGURT SAUCE

Egg Free

Imperial (Metric)	American
1½ lb (680g) coley (or other fish of choice)	1½ pounds coley (or other fish of choice)
4 oz (115g) mushrooms	2 cups mushrooms
3 tablespoons safflower or sunflower oil	3 tablespoons safflower or sunflower oil
2 large potatoes	2 large potatoes
2 large carrots	2 large carrots
sea salt and freshly ground pepper	sea salt and freshly ground pepper

For the sauce:

Imperial (Metric)	American
1 oz (30g) unsalted butter or margarine	2½ tablespoons unsalted butter or margarine
1 oz (30g) wholemeal flour	¼ cup wholewheat flour
¼ pint (140ml) water or stock	⅔ cup water or stock
¼ pint (140ml) natural yogurt	⅔ cup plain yogurt
4 tablespoons grated cheddar cheese	4 tablespoons grated cheddar cheese

1. Wash and skin the fish and place in a greased ovenproof dish.

2. Sauté the mushrooms in a little oil and place over the fish.

3. Peel and slice the potatoes and carrots thinly and sauté in the remaining oil in a large frying pan (skillet) until golden brown, then put around the fish. Season to taste.

To make the sauce:

Melt the butter, blend in the flour and gradually dilute with warm water or vegetable stock. Add the yogurt, and simmer gently for 5 minutes. Pour the sauce over the fish. Cover with grated cheese and bake for 20 minutes in the oven at 375°F/190°C (Gas Mark 5).

Note: Sour cream can be used for this recipe instead of the yogurt.

HOMEMADE PIZZA

The base is very quick to make but you need longer to cook the vegetables, so prepare them first.

Topping:

Imperial (Metric)	*American*
3 *large onions*	3 *large onions*
1 *clove garlic (optional, but nice)*	1 *clove garlic (optional, but nice)*
1 *teaspoon dried mixed herbs*	1 *teaspoon dried mixed herbs*
1 *tablespoon safflower or sunflower oil*	1 *tablespoon safflower or sunflower oil*
2-4 *oz (55-115g) mushrooms*	1-2 *cups mushrooms*
2 *oz (55g) grated cheese*	½ *cup grated cheese*

Peel and chop the onions finely. Crush the garlic. Cook gently with the oil and the herbs in a saucepan for about 30 minutes, stirring occasionally, until they are a soft mass. While they are cooking prepare the base.

Base:

Imperial (Metric)	*American*
2 *oz (50g) margarine*	¼ *cup margarine*
½ *lb (225g) 81%-85% self-raising wheatmeal flour*	2 *cups 81%-85% self-raising wheatmeal flour*
½ *teaspoon oregano*	½ *teaspoon oregano*
2 *free range eggs*	2 *free range eggs*
water to mix	*water to mix*

1. Rub the fat into the flour, add the herbs, then the eggs. Mix to a dough with the water. Roll out thinly and divide into two circles. Place on a greased baking sheet.

2. Spread the prepared onion mixture on top, finely slice the mushrooms and add these, then the grated cheese. Bake for 25 minutes at 425°F/220°C (Gas Mark 7). Will freeze.

Note: Alternative toppings.
2 oz (55g) tin (can) anchovy fillets. Or 4½ oz (125g) tin (can) sardines in oil. With black olives halved and pitted on top. Or add 2 courgettes (zucchini) and 1 aubergine (eggplant), sliced, to the onions and cook together.

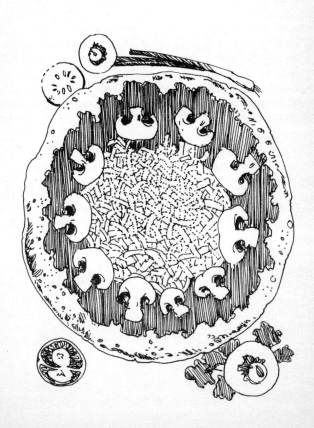

CAULIFLOWER AND BUTTER BEAN CURRY

Grain Free	Gluten Free	Egg Free

Imperial (Metric)	American
2 carrots	2 carrots
½ cauliflower	½ cauliflower
1 potato	1 potato
3 tablespoons sunflower or safflower oil	3 tablespoons sunflower or safflower oil
½ teaspoon ground turmeric	½ teaspoon ground turmeric
1 teaspoon ground cumin	1 teaspoon ground cumin
1 teaspoon ground coriander	1 teaspoon ground coriander
½ teaspoon mustard seeds	½ teaspoon mustard seeds
2 teaspoons fresh grated ginger, or 1 teaspoon powdered ginger	2 teaspoons fresh grated ginger, or 1 teaspoon powdered ginger
¼ teaspoon ground cinnamon	¼ teaspoon ground cinnamon
½ pint (285ml) water	1⅓ cups water
2 oz (55g) dates, chopped	⅓ cup dates, chopped
¼ pint (140ml) natural yogurt	⅔ cup plain yogurt
4 oz (115g) cooked butter beans	½ cup cooked Lima beans

1. Chop the carrots, cauliflower and potato into small pieces. Heat the oil in a pan and add the spices. Next add the chopped vegetables.

2. Cook for 10 minutes stirring well. Add the water and simmer for about 15 minutes, then add the dates, yogurt and cooked butter (lima) beans, and cook for a further 15 minutes.

Note: Serve with brown rice and your choice of side dishes, for example — yogurt, desiccated coconut, chapatis, pitta bread or poppadoms, sliced bananas or mangoes, homemade chutney. Bananas may cause reactions.

FLANS

Serve with baked potatoes and salad. They are also good for picnics. Use wholemeal (wholewheat) or gluten free pastry for the flan case (see page 148 for recipes).

SWEETCORN FLAN

Imperial (Metric)	American
1 8 inch (20cm) flan case, baked blind [this takes 6 oz (170g) wholemeal flour and 3 oz (75g) margarine]	1 8 inch (20cm) flan case, baked blind [this takes 1½ cups wholewheat flour and ⅓ cup margarine]
4 oz (115g) cottage cheese	½ cup cottage cheese
4 oz (115g) sweetcorn	⅔ cup corn kernels
2 free range eggs, beaten	2 free range eggs, beaten
pinch mixed herbs	pinch mixed herbs
pinch sea salt and freshly ground pepper	pinch sea salt and freshly ground pepper

1. Sieve the cottage cheese.

2. Cook the sweetcorn in a little water until soft, then drain and mix well with the other ingredients.

3. Put into prepared flan case and bake in the oven at 375°F/190°C (Gas Mark 5) for 30-40 minutes until set.

MUSHROOM FLAN

Imperial (Metric)

1 9 to 10 inch (23 to 25 cm) flan
   case [using ½ lb (225g)
   wholemeal flour and 4 oz (115g)
   fat], baked blind
½ pint (285ml) milk
3 free range eggs
pinch mixed herbs
sea salt and freshly ground pepper
4 oz (115g) cheese, grated
4 oz (115g) mushrooms, chopped
1 medium onion, finely chopped
a little safflower or sunflower oil

American

1 9 to 10 inch (23 to 25cm) flan
   case [using 2 cups wholewheat
   flour and ½ cup fat] pre-baked
1⅓ cups milk
3 free range eggs
pinch mixed herbs
sea salt and freshly ground pepper
1 cup cheese, grated
1½ cups mushrooms, chopped
1 medium onion, finely chopped
a little safflower or sunflower oil

1. Beat together the milk, eggs, herbs, salt and pepper.

2. Arrange most of the grated cheese over the base of the flan.

3. Sauté the mushrooms and onion in a little oil until soft, then drain and add to the flan. Pour over the egg and milk mixture and sprinkle on the remaining cheese.

4. Bake in the oven at 375°F/190°C (Gas Mark 5) for 30-40 minutes until set and browned on top.

Notes: To vary replace the mushrooms and onion with one of the following:

1. Watercress: one bunch finely chopped.

2. Leeks: 3 medium sized, cut into ¼ inch (½cm) slices, and sauté for approximately 5 minutes.

3. Celery: 1 head of celery and one onion finely chopped.
Sauté for approximately 5 minutes.

4. Shrimps or prawns: 4 oz (115g), added to the milk and egg
mixture, with cottage cheese if desired.
Will all freeze.

For egg free flans: Substitute a 10½ oz (297g) pack of silken tofu for
the egg and cottage cheese or egg and milk. Whisk or liquidize
the tofu until smooth. To give it a yellow colour add ½ teaspoon
of turmeric, and add 1 tablespoon natural soya (soy) sauce for
extra flavour.

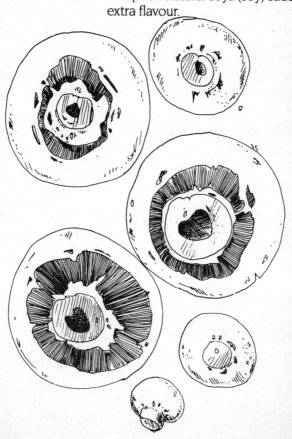

CAULIFLOWER FRITTERS

Milk Free

Imperial (Metric)	American
1 cauliflower	1 cauliflower
wholemeal flour	wholewheat flour
1 free range egg, beaten	1 free range egg, beaten
wholemeal breadcrumbs for coating	wholewheat breadcrumbs for coating
sunflower or safflower oil for frying	sunflower or safflower oil for frying

1. Cook the cauliflower for about 8 minutes until just about tender. Drain.

2. When cooled a little, break off pieces of cauliflower and dip in seasoned flour, egg and breadcrumbs. Fry in a little oil until crisp. Serve with grated cheese if wished.

Note: You can use other vegetables such as turnips, jerusalem artichokes or marrow (summer squash) in the same way.

Remember that the dish will not be milk free if you serve it with grated cheese.

SAVOURY PANCAKES (CRÊPES)

Makes 12

The pancakes (crêpes) can be made in advance and kept in the refrigerator or deep freeze. When you want to eat them, fill them with the chosen filling and reheat in the oven at 350°F/180°C (Gas Mark 4) for 20 minutes.

For the pancakes (crêpes):

Imperial (Metric)

4 oz (115g) 81%-85% plain wheatmeal flour
pinch sea salt
1 free range egg
½ pint (285ml) milk and water mixed
1 tablespoon safflower or sunflower oil

American

1 cup 81%-85% plain wheatmeal flour
pinch sea salt
1 free range egg
1⅓ cups milk and water mixed
1 tablespoon safflower or sunflower oil

1. Make a well in the centre of the flour and salt. Add the egg, then the milk and water mixture. Using a wooden spoon, beat well until smooth.

2. Make the pancakes (crêpes) by oiling the pan with a little oil. Use about 2 tablespoons of the batter for each pancake.

3. Cook until the base is golden brown, then toss and cook the other side for a short time. Repeat until all the mixture is used.

4. Fill with the desired filling, roll up and serve on a heated dish.

SAVOURY PANCAKE (CRÊPE) FILLINGS

1. Celery, Onion and Beansprout.
Sauté together 2 sticks (stalks) of celery, 1 medium onion well chopped, and a handful of beansprouts. Add a dash of natural soya (soy) sauce.

2. Beetroot (Beets) and Cottage Cheese.
1 lb (455g, ½ cup) cooked beetroot (beets), diced.
4 oz (115g, ½ cup) cottage cheese.
chopped parsley or chives.
Combine, heat gently and fill the pancakes (crêpes).

3. Asparagus.
Drain a can of asparagus or use cooked fresh asparagus. Add grated cheese and a knob of unsalted butter.

4. Broccoli.
Cook the broccoli until just soft, add a tablespoon of whipped cream, sea salt, pepper and a dash of lemon juice.

5. Courgettes (Zucchini) or Leeks in a Cheese Sauce.

Imperial (Metric)	American
1 oz (30g) unsalted butter	2½ tablespoons unsalted butter
1 oz (30g) plain wholemeal flour	¼ cup plain wholewheat flour
½ pint (285ml) milk	1⅓ cups milk
3 oz (85g) cheddar or white cheese, grated	¾ cup cheddar or white cheese, grated
sea salt and freshly ground pepper	sea salt and freshly ground pepper
1 lb (455g) cooked, sliced courgettes or leeks	1 pound cooked sliced zucchini or leeks

1. Make the sauce by melting the butter in the pan, add the flour and milk and whisk until it thickens, then stir and simmer for 2 minutes.

2. Stir in the cheese and seasoning. Add the courgettes (zucchini) or leeks. Divide the filling between the pancakes (crêpes).

COURGETTE (ZUCCHINI) MORNAY

Gluten Free	Egg Free

Imperial (Metric)	American
1 lb (455g) courgettes	1 pound zucchini
6-8 oz (170-225g) mushrooms (optional)	3-4 cups mushrooms (optional)

Cheese sauce:

Imperial (Metric)	American
¾ pint (425ml) milk	2 cups milk
4 oz (115g) cottage cheese	½ cup cottage cheese
1½ oz (45g) margarine	3 tablespoons margarine
1½ oz (45g) brown rice flour	3 tablespoons brown rice flour
sea salt and freshly ground pepper	sea salt and freshly ground pepper
bay leaf	bay leaf

1. Wash courgettes (zucchini), trim each end and cut into ½ inch (1cm) slices. Wash mushrooms, and chop or slice. Lay courgettes (zucchini) and mushrooms in an oiled ovenproof dish.

2. Make cheese sauce by putting the milk, cottage cheese, margarine, and flour into a liquidizer and blending until smooth. Heat slowly, stirring all the time until mixture thickens. Simmer for 1 minute and season to taste.

3. Pour over vegetables and add bay leaf. Bake at 450°F/230°C (Gas Mark 8) for approximately 30-40 minutes.

LEEKS À LA POLONAISE

Imperial (Metric)	American
4 large leeks	4 large leeks
safflower or sunflower oil	safflower or sunflower oil
1 oz (30g) unsalted butter	2½ tablespoons unsalted butter
1 heaped tablespoon wholemeal flour	1 heaped tablespoon wholewheat flour
½ pint (285ml) milk	1⅓ cups milk
juice and rind of ½ lemon	juice and rind of ½ lemon
sea salt and freshly ground pepper	sea salt and freshly ground pepper
4 oz (115g) breadcrumbs	2 cups breadcrumbs
4-6 hardboiled free range eggs	4-6 hardboiled free range eggs
1 tablespoon chopped parsley	1 tablespoon chopped parsley

1. Remove roots from the leeks, cut down one side and clean carefully. Cut off the green parts and chop into ¼ inch (½cm) slices. Sauté in a little oil, turning frequently until tender.

2. Make the sauce by melting the butter in a saucepan, then adding the flour and milk. Whisk together and gently heat until the sauce begins to thicken, then stir to make a smooth sauce. Gradually add the lemon juice and seasoning and simmer gently for a minute or two.

3. To prepare the Polonaise topping, fry the breadcrumbs in some oil until crisp and golden. Chop the hardboiled eggs finely, and add to the breadcrumbs with the parsley, lemon rind, salt and pepper to taste.

4. Put the leeks on a warm serving dish, pour the sauce over, and top with the breadcrumb mixture. Garnish with lemon slices and parsley.

Note: You can use other vegetables in the same way. Try courgettes (zucchini), onion, mushrooms or spinach. Some vegetables such as cauliflower, celery, carrots, Jerusalem artichokes and fennel need to be cooked first in a little water. Allow about 1½ lbs (675g) vegetables.

WATERCRESS CHEESY PUDDING

This makes a nourishing, tasty supper or high tea and looks quite pretty when cooked.

Imperial (Metric)

1 bunch of watercress
¾ pint (425ml) milk
1 oz (30g) butter or margarine
4 oz (115g) wholemeal breadcrumbs
4 oz (115g) grated cheddar cheese
sea salt and freshly ground pepper
1 teaspoon made mustard
2 free range eggs, separated

American

1 bunch of watercress
2 cups milk
2½ tablespoons butter or margarine
2 cups wholewheat breadcrumbs
1 cup grated cheddar cheese
sea salt and freshly ground pepper
1 teaspoon prepared mustard
2 free range eggs, separated

1. Wash the watercress well, then chop finely.

2. Heat the milk and butter in a pan, remove from the heat and mix in the breadcrumbs, cheese and seasoning. Add the mustard, egg yolks and chopped watercress.

3. Whisk the egg whites until stiff and fold lightly into the pudding.

4. Put into an oiled pie dish and bake in oven for about 20 minutes at 400°F/200°C (Gas Mark 6), until set and lightly brown on top. Will freeze.

PULSES

How to prepare:

Buy whole pulses if possible as split beans and peas have been processed. Whole beans and peas make it easier to check for broken or damaged ones as well as any grit. Wash well. All beans need soaking except lentils, mung beans, aduki beans and black eye beans. These will cook in 20-40 minutes.

Soak overnight in cold water or in boiling water for 2 hours (with the exception of butter beans as the boiling water will remove their skins). Always cover with plenty of water as pulses swell to more than twice their size. The beans are now ready to cook.

A pressure cooker is a great help since it means that even chickpeas and soya (soy) beans, the longest cooking beans, take only 1-1½ hours. Other beans will take from 10-25 minutes in a pressure cooker, and as a rough guide allow about ⅓ of the usual cooking time (see below).

All beans need to be thoroughly cooked or they will be very indigestible and could make you ill.

Put beans in a saucepan and cover with clean fresh water. Bring to the boil, skim and boil at over 100°C for 10 minutes to destroy toxins. This is not necessary if using a pressure cooker. Do not add salt in cooking as beans and peas may not soften at all. Add a bay leaf instead or herbs and spices of choice. Add salt when cooked if required.

It is always best to cook pulses first before adding to casseroles, savoury dishes, etc. otherwise vegetables can become overcooked. Any pulses dish can be given a complete protein content by adding cooked rice or millet, sunflower or sesame seeds, chopped nuts, wholemeal (wholewheat) flour in the form of bread, pasta etc, or low fat dairy produce. Millet has a mild flavour and needs plenty of seasoning.

There are endless combinations you can try for yourself. Cook more than required of each variety and freeze in small amounts for adding to salads or casseroles.

Note: Dried whole peas may cause a reaction.

COOKING TIMES FOR BEANS

All beans must be cooked until soft and must be seen to boil hard for a minimum of 10 minutes.

Aduki Beans	30-40 mins. (No need to soak)
Black Eye Beans	30-40 mins. (No need to soak)
Butter Beans (Lima beans)	1-1½ hrs.
Canellini Beans	1 hr.
Chickpeas (garbanzo beans)	4 hrs.
Flageolet Beans	1 hr.
Haricot Beans (navy beans)	1½ hrs.
Kidney Beans	1-2 hrs.
Lentils	30 mins. (No need to soak)
Mung Beans	30-40 mins. (No need to soak)
Borlotti Beans (Pinto Beans)	1-1¼ hrs.
Soya Beans (Soy Beans)	3-4 hrs.

RICE

Rice has always been a good substitute for potatoes and is tasty with meat, fish, vegetables and salad dishes.
Although brown rice takes a little longer to cook than white rice, it is well worth the effort. It is better nutritionally since it contains some B vitamins and minerals mainly destroyed in the processing of white rice. It is also a richer source of protein, vitamin E and roughage.
Do not be put off by the look of uncooked brown rice as it gets whiter during cooking, and the flavour and texture are much nicer with the added advantage of not having to rinse the starch off.
Cook 1 part of rice to 2 parts of water and gently boil until soft, about 30-40 minutes. It takes approximately 15 minutes in a pressure cooker.

PASTA

Wholemeal Pasta (made from Durum wheat) is again much better than the refined types, for the same reasons as stated for brown rice. Buckwheat Spaghetti might be tried as a change from wholemeal spaghetti or macaroni etc. It cooks well and does not fall to pieces or stick together.

Cook pasta until 'just tender' and in plenty of water — about 1 pint (570ml) to 4 oz (115g) of pasta. It takes approximately 12 minutes which is roughly 2 minutes longer than the white refined types. 2 oz (55g) dry weight pasta cooks to one generous portion.

Pasta can be served with all kinds of vegetables, cheese or vegetable sauces, grated cheese, or salads. Even fish or meats can be added in small amounts.

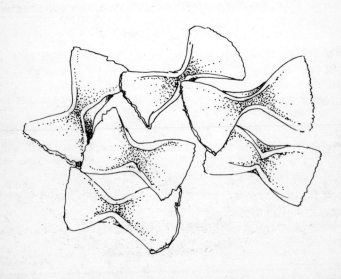

RICE AND CHEESE SAVOURY

Gluten Free

Quick and delicious eaten hot or cold.

Imperial (Metric)

6 oz (170g) whole brown rice, partly
  cooked
½ lb (225g) cottage cheese
1 free range egg
1-2 tablespoons yogurt or milk
2 tablespoons safflower or sunflower
  oil
pinch of mixed herbs
sea salt and freshly ground pepper

American

1 cup whole brown rice, partly cooked
1 cup cottage cheese
1 free range egg
1-2 tablespoons yogurt or milk
2 tablespoons safflower or sunflower
  oil
pinch of mixed herbs
sea salt and freshly ground pepper

1. Mix all the ingredients together and put into an oiled ovenproof dish. Cook at 350°F/180°C (Gas Mark 4) for approximately 30 minutes. Serve hot with vegetables of choice or salad. Will freeze.

Note: Add either of the following before mixing together:-

    1. 1 tablespoon chopped parsley.

    2. Some chopped celery.

CHINESE RICE

Milk Free

For a gluten free recipe use wheat free soya (soy) sauce (tamari).

Imperial (Metric)

½ lb (225g) brown rice
4 tablespoons safflower or sunflower oil
sea salt and freshly ground pepper
3 free range eggs, beaten
½ lb (225g) peeled shrimps
4 oz (115g) mushrooms, sliced
4 oz (115g) cold chicken, cut into strips
4 tablespoons chicken stock
1 tablespoon natural soya sauce

American

1 cup brown rice
4 tablespoons safflower or sunflower oil
sea salt and freshly ground pepper
3 free range eggs, beaten
½ pound peeled shrimps
1½ cups mushrooms, sliced
1 cup cold chicken, cut into strips
4 tablespoons chicken stock
1 tablespoon natural soy sauce

1. Cook the rice.

2. Heat 1 tablespoon of oil in a small frying pan. Season beaten eggs and cook to make an omelette. Remove from the pan, cut into strips and keep warm.

3. Heat 2 more tablespoons of oil and lightly fry the shrimps. Add the mushrooms and chicken. Heat through well, then drain and keep hot with the egg strips. Heat the rice gently in the remaining oil, then add stock, soya (soy) sauce and seasoning to taste. Add all ingredients to the pan and heat through. Put into a hot serving dish and serve immediately.

STIR FRY VEGETABLES IN SWEET & SOUR SAUCE

Milk Free   Egg Free

For a gluten free recipe use a wheat free soya (soy) sauce (tamari).

Imperial (Metric)	*American*
¾ lb (340g) mixed vegetables	¾ pound mixed vegetables
2 tablespoons safflower or sunflower oil	2 tablespoons safflower or sunflower oil
¼ teaspoon sea salt	¼ teaspoon sea salt
1 teaspoon raw cane sugar	1 teaspoon raw cane sugar
1 tablespoon natural soya sauce	1 tablespoon natural soy sauce
2 pinches of ground ginger	2 pinches of ground ginger
3 teaspoons arrowroot, mixed with ¼ pint (140ml) vegetable stock	3 teaspoons arrowroot flour, mixed with ⅔ cup vegetable stock

1. Mix your own vegetables, such as bean sprouts, spring onions (scallions), celery, broccoli, cauliflower, carrots, turnips, mushrooms, cabbage, sweetcorn or courgettes (zucchini). Cut them into very thin slices, or small diagonal chunks or matchsticks.

2. Heat the oil in a pan or wok. Add the 'hard' vegetables first and fry at a high heat for a minute, then add the soft vegetables and fry for 2 minutes.

3. Add the salt, sugar, soya (soy) sauce, ginger and arrowroot mixture. Mix well and cook until the sauce thickens. Serve hot with rice or noodles.

MUSHROOM SOUFFLÉ

Imperial (Metric)

4 oz (115g) mushrooms
1 oz (30g) margarine or butter
1 oz (30g) 81%-85% self-raising
   wheatmeal or 100% wholemeal
   flour
½ teaspoon mustard powder
   (optional)
½ pint (285ml) milk
pinch sea salt and freshly ground
   pepper
3 free range eggs, separated

American

2 cups mushrooms
2½ tablespoons margarine or butter
¼ cup 81%-85% self-raising
   wheatmeal or 100% wholewheat
   flour
½ teaspoon mustard powder
   (optional)
1⅓ cups milk
pinch sea salt and freshly ground
   pepper
3 free range eggs, separated

1. Lightly oil a 2 pint (1 litre) soufflé dish. Trim, chop and wash mushrooms. Cook in a little extra margarine or milk.

2. Melt the margarine in a pan. Add flour, mustard powder, milk and salt and pepper to make a sauce. Heat, stirring or whisking continuously until sauce thickens. Add egg yolks and mushrooms.

3. Beat egg whites until stiff and carefully fold into mixture.

4. Put into soufflé dish and bake at 375°F/190°C (Gas Mark 5) for 40 minutes until well browned. Serve immediately with a green salad.

Note: Replace the mushrooms with any of the following:-

1. 4 oz (115g, 1 cup) grated cheese

2. 4 oz (115g, ⅔ cup) chopped prawns

3. 6 oz (170g, 1 cup) chopped fish.

CORN AND MUSHROOM BAKE

Gluten Free   Egg Free

Imperial (Metric)

1 lb (455g) potatoes and 1 lb
  (455g) parsnips or 2 lb (900g)
  potatoes
½ lb (225g) cottage cheese
1 small onion, grated (optional)
pinch each of marjoram, sweet basil
  and tarragon
4 oz (115g) sweetcorn
4 oz (115g) mushrooms (optional)
safflower or sunflower oil

American

1 pound potatoes and 1 pound
  parsnips or 2 pounds potatoes
1 cup cottage cheese
1 small onion, grated (optional)
pinch each of marjoram, sweet basil
  and tarragon
⅔ cup corn kernels
2 cups mushrooms (optional)
safflower or sunflower oil

1. Cook and mash potatoes and parsnips. Add cheese, onion if used, and herbs. Mix well together.

2. Cook corn in a little water until just soft and sauté the mushrooms, if used, in a little oil.

3. Spread half the mashed mixture smoothly over the base of an oiled ovenproof dish. Arrange mushrooms, if used, and corn over this and top with rest of mashed mixture. Mark lines with prongs of a fork and dot with margarine or brush with oil.

4. Bake in oven at 400°F/200°C (Gas Mark 6) for 30-40 minutes until golden brown. Will freeze.

Notes:

1. Variations: The pie can be made with just sweetcorn or just mushrooms, although mushrooms may be too rich for young children.

2. Serving Suggestion: Serve with leafy green vegetables, i.e., cabbage, greens, curly kale, sprouting broccoli, Brussels sprouts, etc.

VEGETABLE CRUMBLE

Gluten Free   Egg Free

This makes a delicious meal, and you can vary the vegetables according to season. For a milk free recipe, omit the yogurt and lemon and add ¼ pint (140ml, ⅔ cup) of stock instead.

Imperial (Metric)	*American*
2 medium onions	2 medium onions
1 turnip, diced small	1 turnip, diced small
1 carrot, diced small	1 carrot, diced small
1 parsnip, diced small	1 parsnip, diced small
¼ cabbage	¼ cabbage
¼ cauliflower	¼ cauliflower
4 oz (115g) mushrooms	1½ cups mushrooms
4 oz (115g) chestnuts or sweetcorn	¾ cup chestnuts or ⅔ cup corn kernels
safflower or sunflower oil	safflower or sunflower oil
juice of ½ lemon	juice of ½ lemon
¼ pint (140ml) natural yogurt	⅔ cup plain yogurt

Crumble topping:

Imperial (Metric)	*American*
2 oz (55g) soft margarine	¼ cup soft margarine
4 oz (115g) ground brown rice	½ cup ground brown rice
1 oz (30g) ground hazelnuts	3 tablespoons ground hazelnuts
1 oz (30g) ground sesame seeds	3 tablespoons ground sesame seeds
1 teaspoon mixed herbs	1 teaspoon mixed herbs
sea salt and freshly ground pepper	sea salt and freshly ground pepper

1. Prepare the vegetables by chopping them, then sauté gently in the oil until soft (about 10 minutes).

2. Put into a pie dish, mix together the lemon juice and yogurt and pour over the vegetables.

3. Make the crumble by rubbing the fat into the rice or mix with a fork. Add the nuts, seeds, herbs, salt and pepper. Put the crumble over the vegetables and bake at 400°F/200°C (Gas Mark 6) for 30 minutes until golden. Will freeze.

CARROT AND POTATO FLOUR LOAF

Grain Free   Gluten Free   Milk Free

Imperial (Metric)	*American*
6 oz (170g) raw grated carrot	1 cup raw grated carrot
6 oz (170g) celery, grated	1 cup celery, grated
3 oz (85g) soft margarine (milk free)	⅓ cup soft margarine (milk free)
4 oz (115g) soya flour	1 cup soy flour
5 oz (140g) potato flour or butter bean flour	¾ cup + 2 tablespoons potato flour or lima bean flour
2 lightly beaten free range eggs	2 lightly beaten free range eggs
pinch of sea salt	pinch of sea salt
small pinch each of oregano, tarragon and marjoram	small pinch each of oregano, tarragon and marjoram

1. Mix the carrots, celery, margarine and flours well together.

2. Pour beaten eggs over the mixture and add seasoning and herbs. Mix well.

3. Turn into an oiled loaf tin and bake in oven at 325°F/170°C (Gas Mark 3) for approximately 1 hour until set. Will freeze.

Note: Serve with greens or leaf green salad. Good hot or cold.

CELEBRATION NUT ROAST

Milk Free

This is a wonderful nut roast, good enough for Christmas dinner for vegetarians. Eat it hot or cold, or in sandwiches.

Imperial (Metric)

3 tablespoons wholemeal breadcrumbs
6 oz (170g) mixed nuts, eg:
2 oz (55g) cashews or brazils
2 oz (55g) sunflower seeds or peanuts
2 oz (55g) hazelnuts or walnuts
2 carrots, grated
1 large onion
4 oz (115g) mushrooms
4 sticks celery
4 tablespoons parsley, chopped
1 oz (30g) ground sesame seeds
½ teaspoon ground cumin
½ teaspoon celery salt
2 free range eggs
sea salt and freshly ground pepper

American

3 tablespoons wholewheat breadcrumbs
1½ cups mixed nuts, eg:
½ cup cashews or brazils
½ cup sunflower seeds or peanuts
½ cup hazelnuts or English walnuts
2 carrots, grated
1 large onion
2 cups mushrooms
4 stalks celery
4 tablespoons parsley, chopped
3 tablespoons ground sesame seeds
½ teaspoon ground cumin
½ teaspoon celery salt
2 free range eggs
sea salt and freshly ground pepper

1. Grind the breadcrumbs and nuts until fine. Mix together with the grated carrot, and the chopped onion, mushrooms and celery.

2. Add the remaining ingredients, mixing well.

3. Press into an oiled baking tin and bake for 1 hour at 400°F/200°C (Gas Mark 6). Will freeze.

BRUSSELS SPROUTS WITH CHESTNUTS

| Grain Free | Gluten Free | Egg Free |

Imperial (Metric)

2 lb (900g) Brussels sprouts
1 oz (30g) unsalted butter or
   margarine
½ lb (225g) peeled chestnuts
sea salt and freshly ground pepper

American

2 pounds Brussels sprouts
2½ tablespoons unsalted butter or
   margarine
1⅔ cups peeled chestnuts
sea salt and freshly ground pepper

1. Cook the sprouts until just tender, drain, and toss in the butter.

2. Meanwhile, cook the chestnuts in boiling water with a pinch of salt until tender but not broken.

3. Add chestnuts and seasoning to the sprouts. Serve very hot.

CHESTNUT STUFFING

Milk Free

Imperial (Metric)

1½ lb (680g) fresh chestnuts or 1 lb
  (455g) dried chestnuts
2 tablespoons safflower or sunflower
  oil
1 large onion, peeled and chopped
4 oz (115g) wholemeal breadcrumbs
1 large free range egg
2 pinches of dried sage
2 pinches of dried thyme
2 teaspoons of lemon juice
sea salt and freshly ground pepper

American

1½ pounds fresh chestnuts or
1 pound dried chestnuts
2 tablespoons safflower or sunflower
  oil
1 large onion, peeled and chopped
2 cups wholewheat breadcrumbs
1 large free range egg
2 pinches of dried sage
2 pinches of dried thyme
2 teaspoons of lemon juice
sea salt and freshly ground pepper

1. Wash the chestnuts, then split the skins with a sharp knife. Put into a large saucepan of cold water, bring to the boil and simmer for 10 minutes. Drain and remove the skins, then boil the chestnuts for a further 20 minutes, until tender. Remove any remaining pieces of brown skin, put into a bowl and mash. If using dried chestnuts, these must be soaked first overnight, then simmered for 20-25 minutes until soft.

2. Heat the oil and sauté the finely chopped onion until tender but not browned, then add to the mashed chestnuts.

3. Add the remaining ingredients and mix well together.

4. Freeze at this point if desired.

Note: This is adequate to stuff a 8-10 lb (3½-4½kg) turkey. For a *vegetarian roast* make the mixture into a loaf shape, and coat well with wholemeal (wholewheat) breadcrumbs otherwise the pieces of chestnut go hard on the outside. Place on an oiled baking tray and roast at 400°F/200°C (Gas Mark 6) for 40-60 minutes until lightly browned. Serve with Brussels sprouts and roast potatoes.

SPECIAL SAVOURY LENTILS

Grain Free   Gluten Free   Milk Free   Egg Free

This is one of those dishes which actually improves with re-heating so you can prepare it in advance. It's very filling and delicious, just serve it with hunks of wholemeal (wholewheat) bread.

Imperial (Metric)

½ lb (225g) brown lentils
1-1¼ pints (570-710ml) vegetable stock (or use allowed stock cube)
1 bay leaf
1 teaspoon mixed herbs
1 large onion
1-2 or more cloves garlic, crushed
1 carrot, grated
½ lb (225g) mixed vegetables, such as swede, turnip, parsnip, courgette, celery, white cabbage or mushrooms
sea salt and freshly ground pepper
1-2 tablespoons safflower or sunflower oil
1-2 tablespoons lemon juice or to taste

American

1 cup brown lentils
2½-3 cups vegetable stock (or use allowed stock cube)
1 bay leaf
1 teaspoon mixed herbs
1 large onion
1-2 or more cloves garlic, crushed
1 carrot, grated
½ pound mixed vegetables, such as rutabaga, turnip, parsnip, zucchini, celery, white cabbage or mushrooms
sea salt and freshly ground pepper
1-2 tablespoons safflower or sunflower oil
1-2 tablespoons lemon juice or to taste

1. Wash the lentils, look for damaged ones, and check there is no grit. Cook for about 15 minutes in the stock with the bay leaf and mixed herbs.

2. While the lentils are cooking prepare and dice the vegetables.

3. Heat the oil in a pan and sauté the vegetables for a few minutes. Add them to the lentils and simmer altogether for another 15 to 20 minutes, adding more stock if it seems too dry. Season to taste.

4. When the lentils and vegetables are soft remove the bay leaf.

5. Just before serving, add the lemon juice to taste.

DHAL

Grain Free	Gluten Free	Milk Free	Egg Free

This is a major source of protein in an Indian meal, and is delicious served with rice or accompanying a curry.

Imperial (Metric)

½ lb (225g) brown or green lentils
1 pint (570ml) water or vegetable stock
2 tablespoons safflower or sunflower oil
1 teaspoon ground cinnamon
½ teaspoon ground ginger
½ teaspoon ground cumin
½ teaspoon ground coriander
½ teaspoon mustard seeds
sea salt and freshly ground pepper

American

1 cup brown or green lentils
2½ cups water or vegetable stock
2 tablespoons safflower or sunflower oil
1 teaspoon ground cinnamon
½ teaspoon ground ginger
½ teaspoon ground cumin
½ teaspoon ground coriander
½ teaspoon mustard seeds
sea salt and freshly ground pepper

1. Wash the lentils, checking there is no grit, then simmer in the water for ½ hour until they are tender, and the stock or water is almost absorbed.

2. Heat the oil in a pan and add the spices.

3. Cook slowly for a minute or two stirring all the time. Add the lentils, mixing well, then season to taste.

LENTIL ROAST

Grain Free　　Gluten Free

Imperial (Metric)

½ lb (225g) lentils, green or brown
¾ pint (425ml) water or vegetable
  stock
1 bay leaf
1 tablespoon safflower or sunflower
  oil
1 large onion, chopped
1 clove garlic, crushed (optional)
2 sticks celery, chopped finely
1 teaspoon mixed herbs or 2
  tablespoons chopped parsley
4 oz (115g) grated cheddar cheese
1 tablespoon lemon juice
1 free range egg, beaten
sea salt and freshly ground pepper to
  taste

American

1 cup lentils, green or brown
2 cups water or vegetable stock
1 bay leaf
1 tablespoon safflower or sunflower
  oil
1 large onion, chopped
1 clove garlic, crushed (optional)
2 stalks celery, chopped finely
1 teaspoon mixed herbs or 2
  tablespoons chopped parsley
1 cup grated cheddar cheese
1 tablespoon lemon juice
1 free range egg, beaten
sea salt and freshly ground pepper to
  taste

1. Wash the lentils and check there is no grit. Simmer in the water or stock with the bay leaf for 20-30 minutes until all the moisture has been absorbed.

2. Heat the oil in a pan and sauté the chopped onion, garlic and celery until soft but not brown.

3. Put the other ingredients into a mixing bowl, and add the sautéed vegetables to them, then mix together with the lentils. Season to taste.

4. Turn the mixture on to a floured board and form into a roll shape, coating well with flour. Place on to a greased pie dish or baking sheet and bake for 45 minutes until crisp, at 375°F/190°C (Gas Mark 5). Will freeze.

BLACK EYE BEAN LOAF

Milk Free   Egg Free

For gluten free recipe omit soya (soy) sauce and add 1 teaspoon dried mixed herbs or juice of half a lemon. You can obtain wheat free soya (soy) sauce (Tamari).

Imperial (Metric)

4 oz (115g) runner beans or broad beans

4 oz (115g) sweetcorn

1 sliced onion

1 clove garlic (optional)

1 tablespoon sunflower oil

4 oz (115g) beansprouts (optional)

1 tablespoon tahini

1 tablespoon natural soya sauce or use 1 extra tablespoon tahini

2 tablespoons fresh parsley (optional)

½ lb (225g) black eye beans, red kidney beans or haricot beans, cooked

American

⅔ cup green beans or fava beans

⅔ cup corn kernels

1 sliced onion

1 clove garlic (optional)

1 tablespoon sunflower oil

2 cups beansprouts (optional)

1 tablespoon tahini

1 tablespoon natural soy sauce or use 1 extra tablespoon tahini

2 tablespoons fresh parsley (optional)

1⅓ cups black eye beans, red kidney beans or navy beans, cooked

1. Cook runner beans (green beans) and corn in a little boiling water until soft, and drain.

2. Sauté onion and garlic in the oil until soft.

3. Add all the ingredients to black eye beans, adding enough vegetable and/or bean stock to make a soft mixture. Put into an oiled loaf tin and bake in the oven at 375°F/190°C (Gas Mark 5) for 35 minutes. Will freeze.

CHICKPEA AND HARICOT BAKE (GARBANZO BEAN AND NAVY BEAN BAKE)

Grain Free   Gluten Free   Egg Free

For a milk free recipe use sunflower or sesame seeds instead of cheese in the topping.

Imperial (Metric)	*American*
1 *clove garlic (optional)*	1 *clove garlic (optional)*
1 *onion, grated or thinly sliced*	1 *onion, grated or thinly sliced*
1 *carrot, grated*	1 *carrot, grated*
4 *oz (115g) mushrooms (optional)*	1¼ *cups mushrooms (optional)*
1 *tablespoon safflower or sunflower oil*	1 *tablespoon safflower or sunflower oil*
4 *oz (115g) chickpeas and 4 oz (115g) haricot beans, cooked with a bay leaf*	½ *cup garbanzo beans and ½ cup navy beans, cooked with a bay leaf*
good pinch of mixed herbs	*good pinch of mixed herbs*

Topping:

Imperial (Metric)	*American*
1 *oz (30g) grated cheese or 1 oz (30g) sunflower or sesame seeds*	¼ *cup grated cheese or 2 tablespoons sunflower or sesame seeds*

1. Sauté garlic, onion, carrot and mushrooms, if used, in the oil until soft for approximately 10 minutes.

2. Add cooked beans and herbs. Mix well and put into an oiled ovenproof dish.

3. Sprinkle with cheese or seeds and bake in the oven at 350°F/180°C (Gas Mark 4) for 15-20 minutes to heat through and melt the cheese if used. Will freeze.

Note: Other combinations of pulses may be used.

BAKED BEANS

Milk Free	Egg Free

Imperial (Metric)	**American**
1 onion, finely chopped	1 onion, finely chopped
1 tablespoon safflower or sunflower oil	1 tablespoon safflower or sunflower oil
1 oz (30g) brown rice flour	2 tablespoons brown rice flour
½ teaspoon mustard powder	½ teaspoon mustard powder
½ pint (285ml) water or bean stock	1½ cups water or bean stock
1 tablespoon lemon juice	1 tablespoon lemon juice
1 tablespoon black treacle or molasses	1 tablespoon molasses
1 teaspoon raw cane sugar	1 teaspoon raw cane sugar
pinch sea salt	pinch sea salt
½ lb (225g) haricot or soya beans, cooked	1 cup navy or soy beans, cooked

1. Sauté chopped onion in the oil for a few minutes. Mix flour and mustard powder to a smooth sauce with a little of the cold water. Add to onion with all other ingredients.

2. Mix well and simmer gently for approximately 20 minutes. Will freeze.

Notes:

1. Replace lemon juice with white vinegar and replace the black treacle or molasses with ½ tablespoon molasses and ½ tablespoon yeast extract.

2. Add 4 oz (115g, ¾ cup) cooked chestnuts with all other ingredients.

3. Replace brown rice flour with flours to suit your requirements.

BEEFBURGERS

Grain Free	Gluten Free	Milk Free	Egg Free

Imperial (Metric)

½ lb (225g) minced beef
1 small onion, chopped or minced
sea salt and freshly ground pepper
a little chopped parsley (optional)

American

½ pound ground beef
1 small onion, chopped or minced
sea salt and freshly ground pepper
a little chopped parsley (optional)

1. Mix ingredients together.

2. Shape into flat round cakes and grill or fry. A mould may be used for a more professional finish — a plastic food box lid is ideal. Rinse the lid with cold water, fill with mixture and cover with greaseproof (parchment) paper. Roll firmly with rolling pin and gently ease beefburger out of lid. Burgers can be frozen, interleaved with waxed paper.

MUSHROOM BEEFBURGERS

Grain Free	Gluten Free	Milk Free

Imperial (Metric)

1 lb (455g) minced beef
4 oz (115g) finely minced mushrooms
pinch sea salt
1 tablespoon minced onion
1 teaspoon mixed herbs
1 tablespoon soya flour
1 teaspoon sunflower or safflower oil
1 free range egg, beaten

American

1 pound ground beef
1½ cups finely minced mushrooms
pinch sea salt
1 tablespoon minced onion
1 teaspoon mixed herbs
1 tablespoon soy flour
1 teaspoon sunflower or safflower oil
1 free range egg, beaten

1. Mix all the ingredients except the oil, using the egg to bind together.

2. Divide into eight flat cakes. Brush them lightly with the oil and grill until golden brown on both sides. Will freeze.

BROWN RICE CHEESEBURGERS

Gluten Free

Imperial (Metric)

1 large onion, chopped
1 clove garlic (optional)
sunflower or safflower oil for frying
½ lb (225g) cooked brown rice
1 oz (30g) chopped parsley
2 raw grated carrots
1 free range egg
4 oz (115g) grated cheddar or white cheese
sea salt and freshly ground pepper to taste

American

1 large onion, chopped
1 clove garlic (optional)
sunflower or safflower oil for frying
1⅓ cups cooked brown rice
1 cup chopped parsley
2 raw grated carrots
1 free range egg
1 cup grated cheddar or white cheese
sea salt and freshly ground pepper to taste

1. Sauté the chopped onion and crushed garlic in a little oil.

2. Mix all the ingredients together and make into pattie shapes. Fry in oil until crisp, or grill if preferred. These can also be eaten cold, for instance in packed lunches. Will freeze.

CHEESY SAUSAGES

These are delicious. Serve them with baked potatoes and salad.

Imperial (Metric)	*American*
4 oz (115g) cheddar cheese, grated	1 cup cheddar cheese, grated
4 oz (115g) wholemeal breadcrumbs	2 cups wholewheat breadcrumbs
2 tablespoons chopped parsley	2 tablespoons chopped parsley
1 tablespoon chopped chives or spring onion tops	1 tablespoon chopped chives or scallion tops
1 teaspoon mustard powder	1 teaspoon mustard powder
½ teaspoon sea salt and freshly ground pepper	½ teaspoon sea salt and freshly ground pepper
2 free range eggs	2 free range eggs
1 tablespoon water	1 tablespoon water
3 tablespoons safflower or sunflower oil	3 tablespoons safflower or sunflower oil

1. Mix together the cheese, half the crumbs, the parsley, chives, mustard, salt and pepper.

2. Separate the eggs and add the yolks to the mixture. Stir in the water to bind into a ball, adding more water if necessary.

3. Roll into sausage shapes, dip them into the egg whites, then the remaining breadcrumbs. Heat the oil and cook the sausages, turning to brown them evenly.

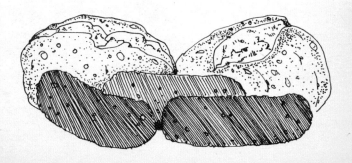

NUT AND MILLET
RISSOLES/PATTIES

Gluten Free   Milk Free

Imperial (Metric)

1 large onion
1 clove garlic (optional)
2 tablespoons safflower or sunflower oil
3 oz (85g) whole millet, cooked with bay leaf
4 oz (115g) nuts, minced or ground (any mixture of sunflower seeds, peanuts, hazelnuts or brazil nuts)
2 oz (55g) mashed potato
2 teaspoons mixed herbs
1 free range egg
pinch of sea salt
maizemeal or rice flour for coating

American

1 large onion
1 clove garlic (optional)
2 tablespoons safflower or sunflower oil
¾ cup whole millet, cooked with bay leaf
¾ cup nuts, minced or ground (any mixture of sunflower seeds, peanuts, hazelnuts or brazil nuts)
¼ cup mashed potato
2 teaspoons mixed herbs
1 free range egg
pinch of sea salt
cornmeal or rice flour for coating

1. Grate or finely chop onion and garlic, if used, and sauté for a few minutes in the oil until soft.

2. Add to millet with rest of ingredients except the egg. Bind with a little of the beaten egg and form into rissoles or patties.

3. Roll in maizemeal (cornmeal) or rice flour. Sauté in the rest of the oil or brush with oil and grill until well browned.

Note: For added flavour use either (a) Juice of ½ lemon. (b) 1 teaspoon yeast extract. (c) 1 tablespoon of soya (soy) sauce (this may contain wheat). (d) A little grated nutmeg.

CURRY POWDER

Grain Free   Gluten Free   Milk Free   Egg Free

The best way is to make up your own, omitting the chillies and cloves (which contain salicylates).

Imperial (Metric)

1 teaspoon fenugreek
1 teaspoon poppy seeds
2 teaspoons cardamoms
1 tablespoon cumin
1 tablespoon turmeric
1 tablespoon mustard seed
1 tablespoon ground ginger
2 tablespoons coriander seed
1 tablespoon black peppercorns

American

1 teaspoon fenugreek
1 teaspoon poppy seeds
2 teaspoons cardamoms
1 tablespoon cumin
1 tablespoon turmeric
1 tablespoon mustard seed
1 tablespoon ground ginger
2 tablespoons coriander seed
1 tablespoon black peppercorns

1. Put the ingredients into a grinder, then store the powder in an airtight tin and use as required.

Note: To make a mild curry use 1 teaspoon per person, or more if you like a stronger flavour.

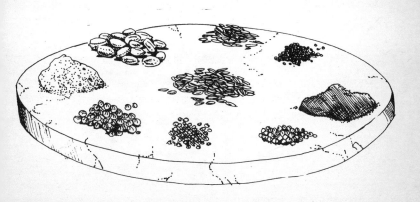

BEEF AND BEAN CURRY

Grain Free   Gluten Free   Milk Free   Egg Free

Imperial (Metric)

1 onion
1 clove garlic (optional)
½ lb (255g) raw minced beef
2 teaspoons curry powder (see recipe on page 83)
1 tablespoon soya flour
1 pint (570ml) vegetable stock
4 oz (115g) haricot beans, soaked overnight

American

1 onion
1 clove garlic (optional)
1 cup raw ground beef
2 teaspoons curry powder (see recipe on page 83)
1 tablespoon soy flour
2½ cups vegetable stock
½ cup navy beans, soaked overnight

1. Sauté chopped onion in a little oil. Add garlic if used, beef and curry powder. Cook stirring for about 5 minutes.

2. Mix flour with a little cold stock and add this with the rest of the stock and beans to pan.

3. Bring to the boil. Boil for 10 minutes then simmer for approximately 1 hour until cooked. Will freeze.

Note: Serve with potatoes and/or other vegetables.

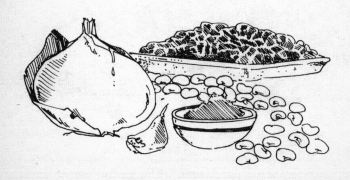

ROAST LAMB WITH GARLIC AND ROSEMARY

Grain Free   Gluten Free   Milk Free   Egg Free

1. Use a leg, a half or whole shoulder of lamb.

2. Crush a garlic clove and rub it over the meat.

3. Insert sprigs of rosemary into the fat of the meat.

4. Roast in a hot oven at 425°F/220°C (Gas Mark 7) allowing 20 minutes per pound plus 20 minutes, or in a moderate oven at 375°F/190°C (Gas Mark 5) allowing 30 minutes per pound plus 30 minutes over.

5. Serve with vegetables, saving the cooking water to make the gravy.

GRAVY

Remove the roast from the tin and keep hot. To make thick gravy pour off most of the fat, keeping about a tablespoon and the brown juices. Add a level tablespoon of permitted flour to the juices and stir over a low heat until the flour browns. Add stock or vegetable water, whisk until it nearly boils, then stir until it thickens. Season to taste.

CASSEROLE OF BEEF

Milk Free   Egg Free

Imperial (Metric)

1½ lb (680g) braising steak
2 oz (55g) wholemeal flour, seasoned
1 aubergine, or 3 sticks of celery
2 onions, sliced
1 clove garlic (optional)
2 carrots, chopped
2 leeks, chopped
4 oz (115g) mushrooms
2 tablespoons safflower or sunflower
  oil
1 bay leaf
½ teaspoon mixed herbs
¼ pint (140ml) stock

American

1½ pounds braising steak
½ cup wholewheat flour, seasoned
1 eggplant or 3 stalks of celery
2 onions, sliced
1 clove garlic (optional)
2 carrots, chopped
2 leeks, chopped
2 cups mushrooms
2 tablespoons safflower or sunflower
  oil
1 bay leaf
½ teaspoon mixed herbs
⅔ cup stock

1. Cut the beef into small cubes and toss in seasoned flour.
2. Chop all the vegetables.
3. Heat the oil in a pan and sauté the meat in it at a high heat until it is browned on all sides. Put on to a separate plate, then sauté the vegetables with the crushed garlic, if used.
4. Put the meat and vegetables into a casserole dish, add the bay leaf and herbs, and pour over the stock.
5. Cover the casserole and cook in a slow oven 300°F/150°C (Gas Mark 2) for 2½ hours.
6. Serve with rice or baked potatoes. Will freeze.

BEEF AND SWEDE (RUTABAGA) LOAF

Grain Free   **Gluten Free**   **Milk Free**

This can be eaten hot or cold, with hot vegetables the first day and salad the next.

Imperial (Metric)

1 lb (455g) minced beef
1 onion, finely chopped
1 carrot, grated
1 small swede, grated (about ½ lb/ 225g)
1 beaten free range egg
1 tablespoon parsley, chopped
sea salt and freshly ground pepper to taste

American

2 cups ground beef
1 onion, finely chopped
1 carrot, grated
1 small rutabaga, grated (about 1 cup)
1 beaten free range egg
1 tablespoon parsley, chopped
sea salt and freshly ground pepper to taste

1. Mix all ingredients together and put into an oiled loaf tin. Alternatively, make into a loaf shape and cook on a baking tray, covered.

2. Cook for 45 minutes in the centre of a moderate oven 350°F/180°C (Gas Mark 4). Will freeze.

SHISH KEBAB

Grain Free	Gluten Free	Milk Free	Egg Free

Imperial (Metric)	*American*
1 lb (450g) piece leg of lamb	1 pound piece leg of lamb
seasoning to taste	seasoning to taste
3 tablespoons safflower or sunflower oil	3 tablespoons safflower or sunflower oil
1 tablespoon lemon juice	1 tablespoon lemon juice
1 clove garlic, crushed	1 clove garlic, crushed
pinch marjoram	pinch marjoram
1 tablespoon chopped parsley	1 tablespoon chopped parsley
1 onion, sliced	1 onion, sliced
bay leaves (optional)	bay leaves (optional)

1. Cut the meat into 1 inch (2cm) cubes. Marinate for 2 hours or overnight in the seasoning, oil, lemon juice, garlic, marjoram and parsley.

2. On four oiled skewers thread the meat cubes, onion slices and bay leaves. Brush with oil and cook under a moderate grill (broiler) for 15-20 minutes, turning about 3 times. If wished you can add button mushrooms or lambs' kidneys. Serve on a bed of plain brown rice with a large green salad.

Note: Alternatively, you could use pieces of steak, with slices of onion and mushrooms.

LIVER LYONNAISE

Milk Free	Egg Free

Imperial (Metric)	American
2 tablespoons safflower or sunflower oil	2 tablespoons safflower or sunflower oil
1½ oz (45g) wholemeal flour	¼ cup + 1 tablespoon wholewheat flour
½ pint (285ml) stock	1⅓ cups stock
1 bay leaf	1 bay leaf
pinch mixed herbs and ground black pepper	pinch mixed herbs and ground black pepper
2 medium onions (approx. ½ lb [225g])	2 medium onions (approx. 1⅓ cups)
2 tablespoons white vinegar	2 tablespoons white vinegar
1 lb (455g) lambs' liver, sliced	1 pound lambs' liver, sliced
seasoned flour for coating	seasoned flour for coating
1 tablespoon safflower or sunflower oil	1 tablespoon safflower or sunflower oil
chopped parsley to garnish	chopped parsley to garnish

1. To make the sauce heat 1 tablespoon oil in a pan, add the flour and allow to brown, then add the stock, bay leaf, herbs and liberal sprinkling of black pepper. Allow the sauce to cook gently for 15 minutes, stirring from time to time and topping up with stock if there is too much evaporation.

2. Slice the onions finely and sauté in 1 tablespoon of oil until golden brown. Drain off excess oil, then add the vinegar and reduce until almost dry. Pass the brown sauce through a sieve on to the onions and allow to cook together for 5 minutes. The sauce should be of a fairly thin coating consistency.

3. Meanwhile, coat the liver in seasoned flour and sauté quickly in the oil on both sides until cooked.

4. Arrange neatly in a dish, pour over sauce and sprinkle liberally with chopped parsley.

LEMON LAMB MEATBALLS

Egg Free

These are tasty and easy to make providing you can obtain some minced lamb. A lot of supermarkets are beginning to do this now, or you can mince your own.

Imperial (Metric)

1 lb (455g) minced lamb
1 carrot, grated
1 potato, washed and grated
1 tablespoon finely chopped parsley
1 teaspoon dried or fresh rosemary
sea salt and freshly ground pepper
2 oz (55g) wholemeal flour or soya flour
¼ pint (140ml) chicken stock
finely grated rind of 1 lemon
2 tablespoons lemon juice
2 tablespoons natural yogurt

American

1 pound ground lamb
1 carrot, grated
1 potato, washed and grated
1 tablespoon finely chopped parsley
1 teaspoon dried or fresh rosemary
sea salt and freshly ground pepper
½ cup wholewheat flour or soy flour
⅔ cup chicken stock
finely grated rind of 1 lemon
2 tablespoons lemon juice
2 tablespoons plain yogurt

1. Mix the lamb, carrot, potato, parsley, rosemary, salt and pepper in a bowl.

2. Make into small balls and coat them in the flour. Put in the refrigerator to make firm.

3. Heat a little oil in a frying pan (skillet) and sauté the meatballs until golden brown.

4. Transfer them to a saucepan and add the stock, lemon rind, and juice. Boil gently for ½ hour.

5. When cooked, combine 2 tablespoons of plain yogurt with the pan juices, and pour over.

Notes:

1. Serve on a bed of brown rice with vegetables of choice.

2. For a grain free or gluten free recipe, use only soya (soy) flour.

DUMPLINGS

Milk Free Egg Free

Imperial (Metric)

4 oz (115g) 81%-85% self-raising
  wheatmeal flour
2 oz (55g) shredded suet
sea salt and freshly ground pepper to
  taste
water to mix

American

1 cup 81%-85% self-raising
  wheatmeal flour
¼ cup shredded suet
sea salt and freshly ground pepper to
  taste
water to mix

1. Add the flour to the suet and seasoning.

2. Mix to a soft dough with the water.

3. Make into balls and add to the casserole for 15-20 minutes.

Notes:

1. To make herb dumplings, just add a teaspoon of mixed
herbs, or to make parsley dumplings, add a tablespoon of fresh
chopped parsley.

2. Vegetarian 'suet' is available from Foodwatch (see list of
suppliers on page 256).

GRAIN FREE DUMPLINGS

Grain Free	Gluten Free	Milk Free

Imperial (Metric)

1 oz (30g) margarine (milk free)
2 free range eggs
1 oz (30g) chickpea flour
1 oz (30g) potato flour
1 oz (30g) soya flour
1 heaped teaspoon baking powder
  (grain free)
pinch of sea salt and freshly ground
  pepper
hot stew, soup or broth

American

2½ tablespoons margarine (milk
  free)
2 free range eggs
1½ tablespoons garbanzo bean flour
1½ tablespoons potato flour
¼ cup soy flour
1 heaped teaspoon baking powder
  (grain free)
pinch of sea salt and freshly ground
  pepper
hot stew, soup or broth

1. Soften the margarine and beat it with eggs until creamy.

2. Gradually stir in flours that have been mixed together well.
    Add nutmeg, salt and pepper. Make sure the mixture is well
    blended. It should be fairly stiff.

3. Drop teaspoons of mixture into simmering stew, soup or
    broth. Cook for 10 minutes and serve.

Note: Other flours may be substituted for the above (see page
235).

SCRAMBLED EGG WITH VEGETABLES

Add vegetables of choice — sweetcorn, runner beans,
beansprouts and mushrooms, etc. to egg mixture and cook as
usual. Serve on bread and butter, toast and/or with salad greens,
e.g. lettuce, watercress.

LEMON CHICKEN

Grain Free	Gluten Free	Milk Free	Egg Free

Imperial (Metric)

1 clove garlic, skinned and crushed
3 tablespoons sunflower oil
sea salt and freshly ground pepper to
  taste
juice of 2 lemons
1 onion, skinned and grated
4 chicken portions, skinned

American

1 clove garlic, skinned and crushed
3 tablespoons sunflower oil
sea salt and freshly ground pepper to
  taste
juice of 2 lemons
1 onion, skinned and grated
4 chicken portions, skinned

1. Mix garlic, oil, seasoning, lemon juice and grated onion together in a bowl.

2. Wash and dry chicken pieces. Place them in a shallow dish and pour over the marinade. Leave to marinate for 1-2 hours.

3. Arrange the chicken pieces in the grill (broiler) pan and pour over the marinade. Grill, basting frequently, under medium heat for 30-40 minutes, or until the chicken is cooked through. Serve with any remaining juices.

VEGETABLE AND POTATO PIE

Put layers of any vegetables, such as marrow (summer squash), courgettes (zucchini), cooked mashed swede (rutabaga) or parsnips, thin slices of onion. Add a little vegetable stock with yeast extract and cover with mashed potato and grated cheese. Serve with a green vegetable or salad.

FISH PIE

Any cooked flaked white fish, in a little homemade parsley sauce. Add sweetcorn (corn kernels) or other vegetables and top with mashed potatoes.

YORKSHIRE PUDDINGS WITH A DIFFERENCE

To basic mixture add —

1. 4 oz (115g, ⅔ cup) of sweetcorn (corn kernels), uncooked.

or

2. 4 oz (115g, ⅔ cup) toasted chopped nuts.

or

3. 4 oz (115g, ⅔ cup) toasted sunflower and sesame seeds.

4. Make individual puddings. Call them 'yorkies' and serve at breakfast.

BREAD AND BUTTER CHEESE PUDDING

Lay alternate layers of bread and butter and grated cheese in an oiled dish. End with layer of cheese. Pour over mixture of 1-2 eggs to ¾ pint (425ml, 2 cups) milk and cook in the usual way. Serve with salad greens, e.g. cress, watercress, lettuce.

4.

SALADS

Fresh salads are full of vitamins and minerals and contain fibre and moisture which aids thirst. Raw salads also aid digestion and cleanse the body. They need to be chewed well like all unrefined foods, and this helps to keep teeth and jaws healthy. Try to have some raw salad daily, as this is better than an occasional large one. If you are not used to eating raw salad foods, gradually build up to a meal by adding one raw item grated in small amounts (1 teaspoon) with other foods.

It is important for everyone, especially children, to obtain adequate vitamin C. If the children cannot eat the fruits containing salicylates they can still get plenty of vitamin C from fresh raw vegetables and grapefruit, lemons, limes etc. Parsley is also rich in vitamin C.

A daily salad could contain any of the following, but always include a leafy green.

Beetroot (beet), grated raw or cooked carrots, grated raw cauliflower, grated raw celeriac, grated raw turnip, grated raw celery, chicory, chives, Chinese leaves (keeps longer than lettuce), cress, endive, fennel (slice finely or chop), garlic, lettuce, onion, parsley, radish (red or white), cabbage (red or white, shredded), spring onions (scallions), Brussels sprouts (shredded), sprouted beans and seeds (beansprouts, alfalfa seeds, etc), tarragon, watercress, young dandelion leaves, young tender spinach leaves (lovely raw in place of lettuce).

Dressings:
These help improve the flavour, food value and digestibility. Vinegar or lemon juice helps to preserve the vitamin C. The oil helps to absorb the fat soluble vitamins, such as vitamin A in carrots.

BEANSPROUTS

These are very cheap and easy to grow, and they are extremely nutritious, containing vitamins, minerals, enzymes, roughage, and a rich supply of polyunsaturated fats.

Put 1 tablespoon (level) of chosen beans or seeds in a clean jam jar and cover the top of the jar with muslin or similar material, to allow for water to filter through. Secure with a rubber band. Keep away from direct heat or sunlight.

Fill the jar with warm water and drain. Repeat 2 or 3 times a day. The seeds will grow from around the sides of the jar. The original volume will increase about 8-10 times before they are ready to eat, in 3 to 6 days.

Discontinue growing after 6 days as flavour will be lost. Discard any seeds that have not sprouted. Rinse and keep hulls as these are nutritionally valuable. Sprouts will keep in the fridge.

They can also be grown in a dark cupboard on blotting paper in a plastic container.

Eat sprouts raw in salads, sandwiches, etc., or add a few (1-2 cups) to casseroles, soups, etc., about 15 minutes before cooking time is up.

Note: Only eat raw sprouted beans and not their seeds as these are likely to make you ill. Most beans can be sprouted except red or white kidney beans.

The most popular are:- Mung beans, alfalfa seeds, aduki beans, green lentils, chick peas (garbanzo beans), whole (uncracked) wheat grain.

FENNEL

The seeds can be used to make tea. They can be cooked with cabbage, or sprinkled on bread rolls or cereals. The feathery leaves can be used in a sauce for fish dishes or chicken. The bulbous root can be thinly sliced and combined with red radishes and a French Dressing, or added to a green salad. They have a delicious aniseed flavour. To cook, boil in water until tender.

SWEETCORN
(CORN KERNELS)

To cook corn on the cob, strip away the husks and the silk from the cobs. Put into boiling unsalted water and cook for 10-15 minutes. Add melted butter and seasoning to taste.

AVOCADO PEARS

Although these are not always to children's taste, they do contain a good supply of vitamins and minerals, and more protein than any other fruit. They also contain up to 25 per cent of unsaturated fat. You can add cubed avocado to salads, tossing the cubes first in oil and vinegar, or lemon juice. Or you can halve the avocado, removing the stone and filling the cavity with prawns (shrimps), or cottage cheese, brushing the surface first with lemon juice to stop discolouration. Let the children plant the stone to grow their own plant.

BAKED YAMS

Also known as Sweet Potato. Scrub and oil the skins. Bake small ones whole or cut large ones into even slices. Cook until tender, 40 to 60 minutes. Serve with butter or margarine.

BOILED YAMS

Yams can be boiled in their skins for 20-30 minutes. Then peel, slice, dot with butter or margarine and season with sea salt and freshly ground pepper.

MASHED YAMS

Cook as for boiled yams. Peel, slice and mash with a little hot milk, butter or margarine and sea salt.

ARTICHOKES

These are delicious served hot with butter or Hollandaise sauce, or cold with a salad dressing, such as mayonnaise flavoured with chopped herbs, prawns, shrimps or mashed tuna fish. You can also use sour cream. First wash the artichoke and cut off stem, then upper leaves. Boil for 45 minutes in salted water with a squeeze of lemon juice, or 7 to 10 minutes in a pressure cooker. Drain and cool, then twist the inner cone of leaves, take out and throw away. Scrape out all the hairy choke with a spoon and discard. Fill the centre with the dressing of your choice. Pull off the leaves, dipping them into the dressing, then eat the soft parts. When the leaves are gone, eat the heart which is delicious.

FUN SALADS

Make faces on a plate. Here are some suggestions, and no doubt you will find many more.
Put a large lettuce leaf on a plate and add the following as required:-

To Make Eyes
Carrot — small piles raw and grated.
Beetroot (beet) — small piles raw and grated.
Radish — thinly sliced.
Mushroom — thinly sliced.
Egg — sliced hard boiled.

To Make a Nose
Celery stick.
Quiche/Flan — small slice (hot or cold).
Savoury sausage — (hot or cold).
Brown rice or pasta — make a long thin pile (hot).
Beans (pulses) — make a long thin pile (hot).
Meat — cut into strips (hot or cold).
Fish — for example, sardine.

To Make Cheeks
Make 2 heaps of any of the following:-
Beetroot (beet) — cooked or raw.
Carrot — raw and grated.
Lettuce heart.
Chinese leaves — shredded.
Cottage cheese or grated hard cheese.

To Make a Mouth
Lettuce — or most of the above.
Savoury sausage (hot or cold).
Sardine.
Scrambled egg — (hot or cold).
Cheese.

To Make Hair
Watercress.
Sprouting beans.
Mustard and cress.
Nuts or seeds and/or dates and figs, chopped.

BANANA SALAD

Grain Free   Gluten Free

---

1. Arrange some mustard and cress, watercress or lettuce on plates. Cut 2 or 3 large bananas in half then in 4 lengthways. Brush with lemon juice.

2. Arrange banana as spokes in a wheel. Put slices of hard boiled egg or small heaps of chopped nuts and dates and/or cottage cheese around plate.

Note: Bananas may cause reactions.

RICE SALAD

Gluten Free   Milk Free   Egg Free

Imperial (Metric)

½ lb (225g) brown rice
2 spring onions, finely chopped
1 small clove garlic, crushed (optional)
2 sticks celery, finely chopped
1 carrot, finely chopped
6 black olives, stoned (optional)
3 tablespoons safflower or sunflower
   oil
1 tablespoon white vinegar
1 teaspoon basil
sea salt and freshly ground pepper

American

1 cup brown rice
2 scallions, finely chopped
1 small clove garlic, crushed (optional)
2 stalks celery, finely chopped
1 carrot, finely chopped
6 black olives, stoned (optional)
3 tablespoons safflower or sunflower
   oil
1 tablespoon white vinegar
1 teaspoon basil
sea salt and freshly ground pepper

1. Boil the rice until tender, but still firm. While the rice is still
   warm add the remaining ingredients and season to taste.

BEAN SALAD

Grain Free   Gluten Free   Milk Free   Egg Free

Imperial (Metric)

½ lb (225g) cooked beans, either red
   kidney beans or a mixture of red,
   white and green flageolets (cook
   separately to preserve the colours)
1 tablespoon sunflower oil
1 teaspoon lemon juice
sea salt and freshly ground pepper to
   taste
1 tablespoon chopped parsley
1 clove garlic, crushed (optional)

American

1 cup cooked beans, either red kidney
   beans or a mixture of red, white
   and green flageolets (cook
   separately to preserve the colours)
1 tablespoon sunflower oil
1 teaspoon lemon juice
sea salt and freshly ground pepper to
   taste
1 tablespoon chopped parsley
1 clove garlic, crushed (optional)

1. Mix all the ingredients well together while the beans are still warm. Chill in the 'fridge before serving.

Note: You can soak and cook larger quantities of beans, then freeze them, and bring out smaller quantities when you fancy a salad. If you mix the beans they look very pretty glistening in the dressing.

CARROT SALAD

Grain Free	Gluten Free	Milk Free	Egg Free

Imperial (Metric)

2-3 carrots, grated
2 oz (55g) chopped walnuts
2 oz (55g) alfalfa sprouts
2 oz (55g) chopped dates

American

2-3 carrots, grated
½ cup chopped English walnuts
1 cup alfalfa sprouts
⅓ cup chopped dates

1. Mix and enjoy.

BEANSPROUT AND CASHEW NUT SALAD

Serves 2-3

Grain Free	Gluten Free	Milk Free	Egg Free

Imperial (Metric)

4 oz (115g) beansprouts
2 sticks celery, sliced
2 carrots
2 oz (55g) cashew nuts
1 teaspoon clear honey
2 teaspoons safflower or sunflower oil
2 teaspoons lemon juice

American

2 cups beansprouts
2 stalks celery, sliced
2 carrots
½ cup cashew nuts
1 teaspoon clear honey
2 teaspoons safflower or sunflower oil
2 teaspoons lemon juice

1. Mix the beansprouts with the celery, grated carrots and cashew nuts.

2. Mix the dressing ingredients and pour over the salad.

GREEN SALAD

Grain Free	Gluten Free	Milk Free	Egg Free

Imperial (Metric)

1 lettuce or half Chinese leaves
1 carton cress
1 tablespoon chopped parsley
1 clove garlic (optional)
1 tablespoon lemon juice
2 tablespoons sunflower oil
freshly ground sea salt and pepper

American

1 lettuce or half Chinese leaves
1 carton cress
1 tablespoon chopped parsley
1 clove garlic (optional)
1 tablespoon lemon juice
2 tablespoons sunflower oil
freshly ground sea salt and pepper

1. Wash the vegetables, and mix together.

2. Rub a bowl with the garlic clove, and add the vegetables. Mix the dressing and season to taste. Pour onto the vegetables and toss to mix.

Note: Serving suggestions:

1. With rice and cheese savoury (see page 63).

2. Pizzas, quiches or pancakes (see pages 48, 51 and 55).

BEETROOT (BEET) MEDLEY

Grain Free	Gluten Free	Milk Free	Egg Free

Imperial (Metric)	*American*
4 raw beetroot, finely grated	4 raw beets, finely grated
4 sticks celery, finely sliced	4 stalks celery, finely sliced
¼ small white cabbage, finely shredded	¼ small white cabbage, finely shredded
2 tablespoons parsley, chopped	2 tablespoons parsley, chopped
2 carrots, finely grated	2 carrots, finely grated
2 cloves garlic, crushed (optional)	2 cloves garlic, crushed (optional)
2 tablespoons sunflower seeds	2 tablespoons sunflower seeds
French dressing (see page 109 but omit mustard)	French dressing (see page 109 but omit mustard)

1. Mix together all the vegetables.

2. Add the garlic to the French dressing and pour over.

BEETROOT (BEET) SALAD

Grain Free	Gluten Free	Milk Free

Imperial (Metric)	**American**
beetroots	beets
hard boiled eggs	hard boiled eggs
spring onions	scallions
French dressing (see page 109 but omit mustard)	French dressing (see page 109 but omit mustard)

1. Peel and slice the beetroots (beets).

2. Chop the onions finely.

3. Fill a salad bowl with alternate layers of beetroots (beets), sliced hard boiled eggs, and onions (scallions).

4. Pour over French dressing.

RED CABBAGE CARAWAY

Grain Free	Gluten Free	Egg Free

This can be eaten hot or cold, and is delicious with roast pork.

Imperial (Metric)	**American**
2 tablespoons safflower or sunflower oil	2 tablespoons safflower or sunflower oil
½ medium red cabbage, finely shredded	½ medium red cabbage, finely shredded
2 pears, cored and diced	2 pears, cored and diced
1 large clove garlic, finely chopped	1 large clove garlic, finely chopped
2 teaspoons caraway seeds	2 teaspoons caraway seeds
1 tablespoon honey or raw cane sugar	1 tablespoon honey or raw cane sugar
1 tablespoon white vinegar	1 tablespoon white vinegar
2 tablespoons natural yogurt	2 tablespoons plain yogurt
sea salt to taste	sea salt to taste

1. Heat the oil and stir in the cabbage, pears, garlic, caraway seeds and honey. Cook for 3 minutes.

2. Mix the yogurt and vinegar, add to the pan and cook for another 3 minutes. Add sea salt to taste.

MELON AND PRAWN SALAD

Grain Free   Gluten Free   Milk Free

Imperial (Metric)

1 melon, cubed
6 oz (170g) peeled prawns
½ pint (285ml) mayonnaise (see page 110)
1 teaspoon grated lemon rind
watercress or lettuce
whole prawns and watercress to garnish

American

1 melon, cubed
1⅓ cups peeled prawns
1⅓ cups mayonnaise (see page 110)
1 teaspoon grated lemon rind
watercress or lettuce
whole prawns and watercress to garnish

1. Mix the melon with the prawns.

2. Add the mayonnaise, and the lemon rind and stir until the melon and prawns are coated.

3. Arrange on a bed of lettuce or watercress. Garnish with whole prawns and watercress.

MELON, GINGER AND CURD CHEESE SALAD

Grain Free	Gluten Free	Egg Free

Imperial (Metric)

1 large ripe honeydew melon
6 oz (170g) curd cheese or Quark
1 level teaspoon ground ginger
   (optional)
1 clove garlic, skinned and crushed
sea salt and freshly ground pepper to
   taste
parsley to garnish

American

1 large ripe honeydew melon
¾ cup pot cheese
1 level teaspoon ground ginger
   (optional)
1 clove garlic, skinned and crushed
sea salt and freshly ground pepper to
   taste
parsley to garnish

1. Cut the melon lengthways into four. Scoop out the seeds.

2. Put the cheese in a bowl and work in the ginger, garlic and seasoning.

3. Pile into the centres of the melon pieces and garnish with parsley.

CAULIFLOWER SALAD

Grain Free	Gluten Free	Milk Free

Imperial (Metric)

1 medium cauliflower
1 firm pear, chopped and cored
2 hard boiled eggs, chopped
2 oz (55g) walnut halves, chopped
¼ pint (140ml) mayonnaise (see
   page 110)
1 tablespoon lemon juice
freshly ground sea salt and pepper to
   taste

American

1 medium cauliflower
1 firm pear, chopped and cored
2 hard boiled eggs, chopped
½ cup walnut halves, chopped
⅔ cup mayonnaise (see page 110)
1 tablespoon lemon juice
freshly ground sea salt and pepper to
   taste

1. Break the cauliflower into florets and wash well.

2. Put all ingredients into a salad bowl, season if wished, and toss well together.

COLESLAW

Grain Free   Gluten Free   Milk Free

Imperial (Metric)

1 small white cabbage, or ½ small
   red and ½ small white cabbage
   (this makes it more colourful)
a few sticks of celery, chopped
small onion, grated (optional)
2 carrots, grated
homemade mayonnaise (see page
   110) to coat

American

1 small white cabbage, or ½ small
   red and ½ small white cabbage
   (this makes it more colorful)
a few stalks of celery, chopped
small onion, grated (optional)
2 carrots, grated
homemade mayonnaise (see page
   110) to coat

1. Shred the cabbage very finely.

2. Add the chopped celery, onion and grated carrot.

3. Mix all the ingredients together with the mayonnaise.

Note: You can add 4 oz (115g, ¾ cup) chopped walnuts (English walnuts) or dates for variety.

HOMEMADE SALAD CREAM

Milk Free

Children often seem to prefer this to the real mayonnaise. You will find it will keep for several weeks in a screw top bottle, if you keep it in the 'fridge.

Imperial (Metric)

2 tablespoons plain 81%-85%
  wheatmeal flour
2 teaspoons raw cane sugar
½ teaspoon sea salt
2 teaspoons dry mustard
1 free range egg
2-3 tablespoons white vinegar
  (increase vinegar if you prefer a
  stronger taste)
¼ pint (140ml) water
safflower or sunflower oil (see method)

American

2 tablespoons plain 81%-85%
  wheatmeal flour
2 teaspoons raw cane sugar
½ teaspoon sea salt
2 teaspoons dry mustard
1 free range egg
2-3 tablespoons white vinegar
  (increase vinegar if you prefer a
  stronger taste)
⅔ cup water
safflower or sunflower oil (see method)

1. Sieve the flour, sugar, salt and mustard into a saucepan.

2. Mix to a paste with the egg, then gradually add the water and vinegar. Cook gently, whisking all the time, until the mixture thickens, then cook for a further 2-3 minutes.

3. Allow to cool, then add enough oil to make a thick coating consistency (about 6-7 tablespoons).

4. Put into a screw top bottle or jar and store in the 'fridge.

FRENCH DRESSING

Milk Free   Egg Free

You can vary the amount of oil to lemon juice or vinegar. Use less oil if you like a sharper flavoured dressing. This makes ¼ pint (140ml, ⅔ cup).

Imperial (Metric)

2 tablespoons white vinegar or lemon
  juice
6 tablespoons sunflower or safflower
  oil
freshly ground sea salt and pepper
½ level teaspoon mustard powder
½ level teaspoon raw cane sugar

American

2 tablespoons white vinegar or lemon
  juice
6 tablespoons sunflower or safflower
  oil
freshly ground sea salt and pepper
½ level teaspoon mustard powder
½ level teaspoon raw cane sugar

1. Put the ingredients together in a bowl and whisk. The oil will separate on standing, so it is a good idea to keep the dressing in a bottle or screw top jar and shake it well before using.

Note: To this you can add fresh herbs, chives or crushed garlic if wished.

MAYONNAISE

Milk Free

For a grain-free and gluten-free mayonnaise, omit the mustard powder. This takes a little while to make as the oil must be added very slowly at first, but it is worth the effort. It is considerably quicker if made in a blender or food processor.

Imperial (Metric)

1 tablespoon white vinegar or lemon juice
⅛ teaspoon mustard powder (optional)
sea salt and freshly ground pepper to taste
2 egg yolks
½ pint (285ml) sunflower oil

American

1 tablespoon white vinegar or lemon juice
⅛ teaspoon mustard powder (optional)
sea salt and freshly ground pepper to taste
2 egg yolks
1⅓ cups sunflower oil

1. Put all ingredients except the oil into a bowl and whisk together.

2. Gradually add the oil, drop by drop, whisking continuously until the mayonnaise is thick.

3. Add a teaspoon of water at the end if it needs thinning.

MUSHROOM MAYONNAISE

Milk Free

For a grain free and gluten free recipe, omit the mustard powder.

Imperial (Metric)

2 oz (55g) fresh white button mushrooms
1 teaspoon lemon juice
1 tablespoon white vinegar
2 free range egg yolks
⅛ teaspoon mustard powder
sea salt and freshly ground pepper to taste
½ pint (285ml) sunflower oil

American

1 cup fresh white button mushrooms
1 teaspoon lemon juice
1 tablespoon white vinegar
2 free range egg yolks
⅛ teaspoon mustard powder
sea salt and freshly ground pepper to taste
1⅓ cups sunflower oil

1. Wash and prepare the mushrooms in ¼ inch (5mm) dice and allow to marinate in the lemon juice and vinegar for 5 minutes, then add to the egg yolks.

2. Mix well, then continue as for plain mayonnaise.

MAYONNAISE WITHOUT VINEGAR

Milk Free

For a grain free and gluten free mayonnaise omit the mustard powder.

Imperial (Metric)

1 free range egg yolk
sea salt and freshly ground black
  pepper
½ teaspoon mustard powder
¼-½ pint (140-200ml) oil,
  depending on thickness required

American

1 free range egg yolk
sea salt and freshly ground black
  pepper
½ teaspoon mustard powder
⅔-¾ cups oil, depending on
  thickness required

1. Mix first three ingredients then add oil very slowly, a few drops at a time. Beat well between each addition.

Note: For garlic mayonnaise: crush 1 clove of garlic, pound in a mortar with a few drops of oil and continue as above.

5.

PUDDINGS

DRIED FRUIT

Sugar occurs naturally in dried fruits and although the vine fruits contain salicylates, dates, figs and pears are safe. Dried bananas may also be safe (use in cakes or puddings).
Dates and figs are very nutritious and high in sugar content so they make good snacks in place of *Mars* bars, etc.
Dried pears have a lovely flavour and a very high iron content. Before use, the pears should be washed well in hot water, especially if sulphur dioxide or mineral oil has been used, then soaked overnight or for at least 6 hours in cold water, although with some crops or varieties this is not always necessary. To cook, simmer gently until soft. Do not boil as this spoils the flavour and breaks up the fruit. You can cook them in the oven, and this takes approximately 1 hour.

FOR JELLIED FRUIT

Add 2-3 teaspoons of agar agar* to 1 lb (455g) of any safe fruit, dried or fresh. Mix agar agar with a little water and add to fruit either before or immediately after stewing. Stir well. This will set soft or firm depending on how much agar agar is used.

Note: Gelatine usually contains the preservative sulphur dioxide. However, preservative free gelatine is available from Foodwatch (see list of suppliers on page 256).

*Agar agar is a natural substitute for gelatine, and is full of vitamins and minerals. Only a small amount is required, and it sets quickly. It is suitable for savoury or sweet dishes, and is available from health food stores.

FRESH FRUIT SALAD

Grain Free	Gluten Free	Milk Free	Egg Free

Imperial (Metric)

1 grapefruit, cut into small pieces
2 pears, cored and sliced or ½ small
  melon, cubed
1 small tin of pineapple in its own
  juice, or fresh pineapple
1 tin guavas (rinse off syrup)
1 pomegranate (optional)
1 tablespoon honey
4 fl oz (120ml) water

American

1 grapefruit, cut into small pieces
2 pears, cored and sliced or ½ small
  melon, cubed
1 small can of pineapple in its own
  juice, or fresh pineapple
1 can guavas (rinse off syrup)
1 pomegranate (optional)
1 tablespoon honey
½ cup water

1. Put the grapefruit into a bowl. Add the pears or melon and mix well to prevent discolouration. Add the other fruit.

2. Dissolve the honey in the water and pour over.

FIG AND YOGURT DESSERT

Grain Free	Gluten Free	Egg Free

Imperial (Metric)

4 oz (115g) figs
2 pears
¼ pint (140ml) natural yogurt

American

1 cup figs
2 pears
⅔ cup plain yogurt

1. Stew the fruit in a little water and when soft, liquidize together, or mash and purée.

2. Add the yogurt, mix well and serve in individual dishes.

MANGO TOFU SURPRISE

Serves 2-3

| Grain Free | Gluten Free | Milk Free | Egg Free |

This is simple to make and high in protein.

Imperial (Metric)

2 mangoes
1 10½ oz (297g) pack silken tofu
2 tablespoons clear honey
2 teaspoons lemon juice

American

2 mangoes
1¼ cups silken tofu
2 tablespoons clear honey
2 teaspoons lemon juice

1. Skin the mangoes, then scrape off the fruit from the stone with a sharp knife.

2. Put the fruit, tofu, honey and lemon juice in a liquidizer and blend together. If you do not have a liquidizer, put the fruit through a sieve then whisk the ingredients together.

RHUBARB FOOL

| Grain Free | Gluten Free |

Imperial (Metric)

1 lb (455g) rhubarb, chopped
raw cane sugar to taste
1 pint (570ml) homemade custard
(see pages 136-37)
natural vanilla essence (or use vanilla
flavoured sugar)

American

1 pound rhubarb, chopped
raw cane sugar to taste
2½ cups homemade custard (see
pages 136-37)
natural vanilla essence (or use vanilla
flavoured sugar)

1. Cook the rhubarb for 5-10 minutes until soft, adding sugar to taste. Purée the rhubarb when cool and mix with the custard. Chill and serve in individual dishes.

Alternatively make it into a rhubarb ice cream, by freezing it for 30 minutes. Then take it out of the freezer and beat well, return it and freeze until set.

PEAR AND FIG OATMEAL CRUMBLE

Egg Free

This is a lovely crumble which will adapt to other fruit of choice.

Imperial (Metric)	American
3 pears	3 pears
½ grapefruit (fruit and juice)	½ grapefruit (fruit and juice)
4 oz (115g) cooked figs	1 cup cooked figs

Crumble:

Imperial (Metric)	American
3 oz (85g) wholemeal flour	¾ cup wholewheat flour
3 oz (85g) rolled oats	¾ cup rolled oats
2 oz (55g) soft natural raw cane sugar	⅓ cup soft natural raw cane sugar
2 oz (55g) margarine	¼ cup margarine
1 teaspoon ground cinnamon	1 teaspoon ground cinnamon
2 oz (55g) hazelnuts, chopped and roasted	½ cup hazelnuts, chopped and roasted

1. Slice the pears and put in a pie dish. Add the juice and fruit of the grapefruit, then the figs.

2. To make the crumble, combine the flour, oats, sugar, margarine and cinnamon in a bowl. Rub in the margarine, then fork in the hazelnuts.

3. Sprinkle the mixture over the fruit and bake for 40 minutes at 350°F/180°C (Gas Mark 4), or until the crumble is browned. Serve hot or cold with custard, yogurt or ice cream.

SOYA CRUMBLE

Grain Free	Gluten Free	Milk Free	Egg Free

Imperial (Metric)

½ lb (225g) soya flour
4 tablespoons safflower or sunflower
    oil
grated rind of ½ lemon
pinch sea salt
cold water as required

American

2 cups soy flour
4 tablespoons safflower or sunflower
    oil
grated rind of ½ lemon
pinch sea salt
cold water as required

1. Mix flour with oil, lemon rind and salt. Mix well with a fork. Add just enough cold water to hold dough together but let it stay crumbly.

2. Press into a 9-inch (23cm) flan dish and bake at 350°F/180°C (Gas Mark 4) for 15 minutes.

3. When cold crumble over any stewed or fresh 'safe' fruit.

Note: For a sweet crumble add 2 oz (55g, ⅓ cup) of raw cane sugar.

DATE AND NUT SLICE

Egg Free

Imperial (Metric)

6 oz (170g) margarine
¾ lb (340g) 81%-85% self-raising
   wheatmeal flour
3 tablespoons cold water

American

⅔ cup margarine
3 cups 81%-85% self-raising
   wheatmeal flour
3 tablespoons cold water

For the filling:

Imperial (Metric)

¾ lb (340g) dates or figs
¼ pint (140ml) water
4 oz (115g) chopped walnuts or
   hazelnuts

American

2½ cups dates or figs
⅔ cup water
¾ cup chopped English walnuts or
   hazelnuts

1. Grease a medium Swiss roll tin.

2. Make the pastry by rubbing the fat into the flour and adding the water to make a dough. Chill in the 'fridge while making the filling.

3. Cut the dates or figs into small pieces and simmer gently in the water for 5-10 minutes until puréed.

4. Roll out half the dough on a floured board and line the tin. Add chopped nuts to the dates or figs mixture and spread on top of pastry. Roll out the remaining dough and place on top. Trim and press down firmly, then prick with a fork.

5. Bake for 20 minutes at 350°F/180°C (Gas Mark 4).

6. Cool in the tin and cut into slices. Eat for tea, or serve hot with custard or yogurt.

SPICED RHUBARB JELLY

Grain Free	Gluten Free	Milk Free	Egg Free

Imperial (Metric)

1 lb (455g) rhubarb
¾ pint (425ml) water
raw cane sugar or honey to taste
1 teaspoon ground cinnamon
natural red colouring made from
   beetroot juice or 1 hibiscus tea bag
   (this is optional)
2 teaspoons agar agar (available from
   health shops)

American

1 pound rhubarb
2 cups water
raw cane sugar or honey to taste
1 teaspoon ground cinnamon
natural red coloring made from beet
   juice or 1 hibiscus tea bag (this is
   optional)
2 teaspoons agar agar (available from
   health shops)

1. Stew the rhubarb with water, sugar, cinnamon and colouring, if used, until it becomes a purée.

2. Mix agar agar with a little water and stir into purée.

3. Remove from the heat and allow to cool slightly before putting it into dishes.

4. Serve with whipped cream or tofu whipped cream.

Note: You can add 4-6 oz (115-170g, 1 cup) dates to the rhubarb when cooking to make a change.

BAKED MARZIPAN PEARS

Serves 2

Grain Free Gluten Free Milk Free

Imperial (Metric)

2 oz (55g) ground hazelnuts
2 teaspoons lemon juice
yolk of a free range egg
2 teaspoons honey
2 large pears (comice are good for this recipe)

American

½ cup ground hazelnuts
2 teaspoons lemon juice
yolk of a free range egg
2 teaspoons honey
2 large pears

1. Make the marzipan mixture by mixing together the hazelnuts, lemon juice, egg yolk and honey.

2. Remove the stalks from the pears, then with a teaspoon or apple corer, remove the core from the top, keeping the pears whole.

3. Stuff with the marzipan and bake in a moderate oven at 350°F/180°C (Gas Mark 4) for 30 minutes. Serve with custard sauce (page 137).

CAROB PEAR PUDDING

Milk Free

Imperial (Metric)	**American**
2 free range eggs	2 free range eggs
2 oz (55g) muscovado sugar	⅓ cup muscovado sugar
2 oz (55g) 81%-85% wheatmeal self-raising flour	½ cup 81%-85% wheatmeal self-raising flour
2 oz (55g) carob powder	½ cup carob powder
1 lb (455g) dessert pears	1 pound dessert pears
a few walnuts or hazelnuts, chopped	a few English walnuts or hazelnuts, chopped

1. Whisk together eggs and sugar at maximum speed in electric mixer until double in bulk and light in colour. If you do not have a mixer, separate the eggs and whisk the whites until stiff, then beat in the yolks and sugar.

2. Sift the flour and fold into the egg mixture, including any bran left in the sieve. Add a little water to the carob powder, and fold into the sponge mixture.

3. Peel and thinly slice the pears and put into a shallow greased baking dish. Pour sponge mixture on top. Scatter with chopped walnuts (English walnuts) or hazelnuts if liked and bake in the oven at 400°F/200°C (Gas Mark 6) for 30-40 minutes, until firm to touch. Serve with cream, yogurt, or tofu whipped cream.

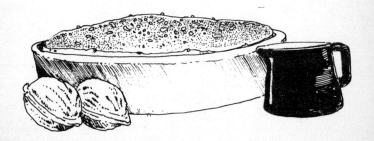

PEAR 'CLAFOUTIS'
(BASED ON A FRENCH RECIPE)

Gluten Free

Imperial (Metric)

1 lb (455g) pears
4-5 tablespoons pineapple or
   grapefruit juice
4 oz (115g) raw cane sugar
2 free range egg yolks
1 whole egg
4 oz (115g) brown rice flour
4 oz (115g) margarine, melted
few drops natural vanilla essence
⅓ pint (200ml) milk

American

1 pound pears
4-5 tablespoons pineapple or
   grapefruit juice
⅔ cup raw cane sugar
2 free range egg yolks
1 whole egg
¾ cup brown rice flour
½ cup margarine, melted
few drops natural vanilla essence
¾ cup milk

1. Slice pears thinly and put into an oiled ovenproof dish. Spoon over juice to stop discolouration.

2. Beat the sugar and egg yolks until mixture becomes white. Add the whole egg and beat again. Add flour and beat in, then the melted margarine, and essence. At the last moment add the milk. Mix well.

3. Pour mixture over the fruit. Cook in a pre-heated oven at 425°F/220°C (Gas Mark 7) for 30-45 minutes. Eat hot or cold.

BANANA SWEET

Grain Free	Gluten Free	Milk Free	Egg Free

Peel one banana per person. Roll in a little melted clear honey and coat with chopped mixed nuts. Serve as it is or with yogurt, etc.

Note: Banana may cause reactions.

DRIED PEARS WITH GINGERBREAD TOPPING

Imperial (Metric)	American
½ lb (225g) dried pears	1½ cups dried pears

Gingerbread:

Imperial (Metric)	American
3 oz (85g) black treacle or molasses	3 tablespoons molasses
2 oz (55g) margarine	¼ cup margarine
1 oz (30g) raw cane sugar	2½ tablespoons raw cane sugar
4 oz (115g) plain wholemeal flour	1 cup plain wholewheat flour
1 teaspoon baking powder	1 teaspoon baking powder
½ teaspoon bicarbonate of soda	½ teaspoon baking soda
1 teaspoon ground ginger	1 teaspoon ground ginger
1 free range egg	1 free range egg
5 tablespoons milk	5 tablespoons milk

1. Rinse the dried pears in boiling water to help wash off the preservative. Leave to soak in fresh water for several hours, then simmer until soft.

2. Warm the treacle, margarine and sugar in a saucepan. Sift the dry ingredients and make a well in the centre. Add the treacle mixture, beaten egg and milk.

3. Put the pears at the bottom of an ovenproof dish with no liquid. Spread the gingerbread mixture over the top.

4. Bake for 1-1¼ hours at 350°F/180°C (Gas Mark 4) until it is firm to touch.

5. Serve with custard sauce (see page 137) or yogurt.

Note: Replace dried pears with 1-1½ lb (455-680g) fresh pears, cored and sliced.

BUTTERSCOTCH BANANAS

Grain Free   Gluten Free   Egg Free

Imperial (Metric)

6 bananas
1 oz (30g) butter
1 oz (30g) soft raw cane sugar
grated rind and juice of 2 lemons

American

6 bananas
2½ tablespoons butter
2 tablespoons soft raw cane sugar
grated rind and juice of 2 lemons

1. Peel bananas. Cut in half lengthways. Place in oiled ovenproof dish and sprinkle with lemon.

2. Dot with butter and dredge with sugar.

3. Cover and bake in the oven at 350°F/180°C (Gas Mark 4) for 20 minutes.

4. Serve with cream or yogurt, etc.

Note: Bananas may cause reactions.

COCONUT SUPREME

Gluten Free

Imperial (Metric)

2 oz (55g) whole millet
¾ pint (425ml) water
2-3 medium to large pears, stewed
   and sweetened to taste
2 oz (55g) margarine
2 oz (55g) soft raw cane sugar
2 free range eggs
4 oz (115g) desiccated coconut

American

¼ cup whole millet
2 cups water
2-3 medium to large pears, stewed
   and sweetened to taste
¼ cup margarine
⅓ cup soft raw cane sugar
2 free range eggs
1⅓ cups desiccated coconut

1. Cook the millet in water until soft and fluffy. Put into an oiled 1 pint (570ml) pie dish. Place the pears on top.

2. Cream the margarine and sugar, add the well beaten eggs, and fold in the coconut.

3. Spread on top of the pears.

4. Cook in a slow oven at 300°F/150°C (Gas Mark 2) for 30-35 minutes until golden brown.

CHESTNUT DELIGHT

Serves 2-3

Grain Free   Gluten Free

Imperial (Metric)	*American*
4 oz (115g) chestnut purée	1¼ cups chestnut purée
2 egg yolks, free range	2 egg yolks, free range
1 large tablespoon clear honey	1 large tablespoon clear honey
4 tablespoons water	4 tablespoons water
1 teaspoon natural vanilla essence	1 teaspoon natural vanilla essence
¼ pint (140ml) natural yogurt	⅔ cup plain yogurt

1. Put the chestnut purée, egg yolks, honey and water into a double saucepan, or a basin standing in a saucepan of water.

2. Whisk the mixture until it becomes a thick sauce.

3. Leave until cold then whisk in the vanilla essence and yogurt.

4. Serve as a pudding, or you can freeze it to make ice cream.

LIME MOUSSE

Gluten Free   Milk Free

***

Imperial (Metric)

2 oz (55g) ground rice
3 oz (85g) raw cane sugar
2 free range eggs, separated
1 pint (570ml) boiling water
juice of 1-2 limes

American

3 tablespoons ground rice
½ cup raw cane sugar
2 free range eggs, separated
2½ cups boiling water
juice of 1-2 limes

1. Mix ground rice into a smooth paste with a little water. Add sugar and beaten egg yolks. Mix well together then add the boiling water. Bring gently to the boil again, and cook for 5 minutes, stirring most of the time.

2. Whisk egg whites stiffly and fold quickly into the mixture. Stir in the lime juice. Pour into a glass dish or individual dishes. Needs to be eaten the same day.

Note: Uncooked egg white destroys biotin but this method cooks it slightly.

INSTANT LEMON PUDDING

Grain Free   Gluten Free   Milk Free

***

Imperial (Metric)

½ pint (285ml) warm water
3 teaspoons agar agar
2 free range eggs, lightly boiled
1-2 tablespoons honey
1-2 tablespoons lemon juice
¼ pint (140ml) safflower or
    sunflower oil
desiccated coconut (optional)

American

1⅓ cups warm water
3 teaspoons agar agar
2 free range eggs, lightly boiled
1-2 tablespoons honey
1-2 tablespoons lemon juice
⅔ cup safflower or sunflower oil
desiccated coconut (optional)

1. Place the water and agar agar in a liquidizer and blend until agar agar has dissolved and the liquid is foaming.

2. Add the eggs, honey and lemon juice. Liquidize again.

3. Finally add the oil a little at a time until mixture thickens.

4. Pour into wetted moulds and chill.

To serve, garnish with desiccated coconut, or finely chopped nuts.

UNCOOKED LEMON CHEESECAKE

Imperial (Metric)	*American*
6 oz (170g) *digestive biscuits or semi sweet or ryvita biscuits*	1¾ *cups Graham crackers or semi sweet or ryvita biscuits*
3 oz (85g) *unsalted butter*	⅓ *cup unsalted butter*
½ lb (225g) *cottage cheese*	1 *cup cottage cheese*
6 tablespoons *homemade lemon curd*	6 tablespoons *homemade lemon curd*
¼ pint (140ml) *double cream, whipped*	⅔ *cup heavy cream, whipped*

1. Crush digestive biscuits (Graham crackers) between 2 pieces of greaseproof (parchment) paper with a rolling pin. Melt butter and mix with biscuit crumbs. Press into a fluted flan tin, or flan ring on a flat dish. Leave to cool until firm.

2. Meanwhile, sieve cottage cheese, beat in 4 tablespoons of lemon curd, and fold in the cream.

3. Smooth on to prepared flan, and leave to set. Spread the rest of the lemon curd on top, slightly warmed if necessary, before serving.

BAKED LEMON PUDDING
(with its own sauce)

Imperial (Metric)	American
2 oz (55g) margarine	⅓ cup margarine
3 oz (85g) raw cane sugar	½ cup raw cane sugar
2 oz (55g) 81%-85% wheatmeal self-raising flour	½ cup 81%-85% wheatmeal self-raising flour
1 large lemon	1 large lemon
2 free range eggs, separated	2 free range eggs, separated
½ pint (285ml) milk	1⅓ cups milk

1. Put margarine, sugar, flour, grated lemon rind, and 3 tablespoons of lemon juice in the liquidizer. Add the egg yolks and milk and whisk together.

2. Whisk the egg whites separately until stiff, then fold in to the mixture from the liquidizer.

3. Turn into an oiled 2 pint (1 litre) pie dish. Put pie dish in a larger shallow dish of cold water and bake for 45-60 minutes at 350°F/180°C (Gas Mark 4) until golden brown and lightly set. A sauce forms below a light sponge. Delicious!

Note: If you do not own a liquidizer, cream the margarine with the grated lemon rind. Add the sugar and cream again. Stir in egg yolks, flour and lemon juice, then slowly add the milk like a batter. Continue as described above.

PINEAPPLE UPSIDE DOWN CAKE

Imperial (Metric)

2 tablespoons clear honey
4-6 slices of pineapple, fresh or
   canned in own juice (keep juice)
1 tablespoon muscovado sugar
6 oz (170g) margarine
3 oz (85g) muscovado sugar
3 free range eggs
6 oz (170g) wholemeal self-raising
   flour
2 oz (55g) carob powder (optional)
milk, yogurt or pineapple juice

American

2 tablespoons clear honey
4-6 slices of pineapple, fresh or
   canned in own juice (keep juice)
1 tablespoon muscovado sugar
⅔ cup margarine
½ cup muscovado sugar
3 free range eggs
1½ cups wholewheat self-raising flour
½ cup carob powder (optional)
milk, yogurt or pineapple juice

1. Well oil an 8-inch (20cm) round cake tin. Spread honey over base and arrange pineapple rings on top. Sprinkle 1 tablespoon of sugar over pineapple.

2. Cream margarine and sugar until light and fluffy. Gradually add beaten eggs and fold in sifted flour and carob powder, if used, mixed together.

3. Add enough liquid to give dropping consistency. Spread over pineapple. Bake at 350°F/180°C (Gas Mark 4) for 1 hour until firm to the touch.

4. Carefully turn out on to a plate and serve hot with custard sauce etc. (see page 137), or eat cold with yogurt or cream, etc.

Note: Replace pineapple with 2 to 3 pears, halved. Fill the core hole with chopped dates or figs.

PINEAPPLE CREAM

Grain Free   Gluten Free   Egg Free

Imperial (Metric)

1 tablespoon arrowroot
¾ pint (425ml) pineapple juice
1 teaspoon lemon juice
2 teaspoons honey
small tin of pineapple in its own juice
4 tablespoons whipped cream

American

1 tablespoon arrowroot flour
2 cups pineapple juice
1 teaspoon lemon juice
2 teaspoons honey
small can of pineapple in its own juice
4 tablespoons whipped cream

1. Mix the arrowroot with some of the juice then add to the rest of the juice.

2. Heat the mixture gently in a pan, stirring all the time, until it thickens.

3. Cook gently for a minute or two, then remove from the heat.

4. Stir in the lemon juice, honey, and chopped pineapple pieces, saving one or two for decoration.

5. Allow the mixture to cool, then fold in the whipped cream and put into individual dishes. Decorate with the remaining pineapple.

Note: 2 oz (55g, 3 tablespoons) brown rice flour may be used in place of arrowroot, but the recipe will not be grain free.

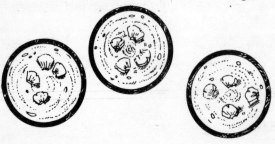

PINEAPPLE MERINGUE PUDDING

For a gluten free recipe, use brown rice flour instead of
wholemeal (wholewheat) flour.

Imperial (Metric)

2 oz (55g) margarine or unsalted
 butter
2 oz (55g) 81%-85% plain
 wheatmeal flour or brown rice flour
¾ pint (425ml) milk
2 oz (55g) raw cane sugar
2 free range eggs, separated
1 small tin pineapple chunks (in own
 juice)

American

¼ cup margarine or unsalted butter
½ cup 81%-85% plain wheatmeal
 flour or 3 tablespoons brown rice
 flour
2 cups milk
⅓ cup raw cane sugar
2 free range eggs, separated
1 small can pineapple chunks (in
 own juice)

1. Melt the butter in a pan, stir in the flour, add the milk and
 whisk until sauce thickens.

2. Take from the heat, and add the sugar, beaten egg yolks and
 pineapple with a little juice. Stir quickly.

3. Pour into an oiled pie dish and bake in the oven at
425°F/220°C (Gas Mark 7) for 20 minutes, or until the pudding
 is set. Allow to cool.

4. Whisk the egg whites until stiff, adding a little sugar, then
spread on top and brown for about 15 minutes in the oven at
275°F/140°C (Gas Mark 1).

PINEAPPLE JELLY

Grain Free	Gluten Free	Milk Free	Egg Free

Imperial (Metric)

2 level teaspoons agar agar
½ pint (285ml) fresh pineapple juice
½ lb (225g) tin pineapple pieces in
their own juice (or fresh pineapple
and ¼ pint [140ml] juice)

American

2 level teaspoons agar agar
1⅓ cups fresh pineapple juice
⅔ cup canned pineapple pieces in
their own juice (or fresh pineapple
and ⅔ cup juice)

1. Mix the agar agar with a little cold pineapple juice.

2. Heat the remaining juice, including the juice drained from the can of pineapple. Stir in the agar agar.

3. Place the pineapple pieces in a jelly mould, or 4-6 smaller dishes. Pour the hot juice over and leave to set.

4. Serve with whipped cream or tofu whipped cream.

JUNKET

Grain Free	Gluten Free	Egg Free

Imperial (Metric)

1 pint (570ml) milk
1 teaspoon vegetarian rennet
2 teaspoons raw cane sugar
a few drops of natural lime or vanilla
essence or a little grated nutmeg

American

2½ cups milk
1 teaspoon vegetarian rennet
2 teaspoons raw cane sugar
a few drops of natural lime or vanilla
essence or a little grated nutmeg

1. Warm the milk to blood heat (feels warm to the little finger) add rennet, sugar to taste, and essence if used.

2. Stir carefully and pour into dish or dishes. Add nutmeg if used. Keep in a warm place to set.

3. Serve cold on its own or with fruit.

Notes:

1. Can also be decorated with finely chopped nuts or desiccated coconut instead of nutmeg.

2. Essences which do not contain artificial additives are based in alcohol.

3. Vegetarian rennet is available from health food shops.

LEMON SAUCE

Grain Free	Gluten Free	Milk Free	Egg Free

Imperial (Metric)

1 oz (25g) soya flour
1 oz (25g) chickpea or other grain
  free flour
½ pint (285ml) water
grated rind and juice of 1 lemon
2 tablespoons raw cane sugar

American

¼ cup soy flour
1½ tablespoons garbanzo or other
  grain free flour
1⅓ cups water
grated rind and juice of 1 lemon
2 tablespoons raw cane sugar

1. Mix flours with a little of the cold water.

2. Heat remainder of the water and pour slowly over mixture, stirring all the time. Return to the pan, add lemon rind and juice, and sugar and simmer for 3-5 minutes. Taste and add more sugar if required.

MILLET MILK PUDDING

Gluten Free

Imperial (Metric)

3-4 oz (85-115g) dried pears
2 oz (55g) millet, whole or flaked
1 pint (570ml) milk
1 bay leaf (optional)

American

½-¾ cup dried pears
¼ cup whole millet or 1 scant cup
    millet flakes
2½ cups milk
1 bay leaf (optional)

1. Cut the pears into small pieces with scissors. Do not use the core unless soft. Wash the millet (whole only). Wash the pears through a sieve with hot water to help remove preservative.

2. Heat the milk. Add the millet and pears to hot milk. Bring to the boil and simmer until soft and thick.

3. Transfer to an oiled ovenproof dish. Lay the bay leaf on the top if used and cook at 350°F/180°C (Gas Mark 4) for 30-40 minutes until set and well browned.

Notes:

1. Use chopped dates or figs instead of dried pears, but do not cook these in the milk first. Arrange the figs and dates in the oiled ovenproof dish and pour the hot milk and softened millet on top.

2. Added sugar should not be necessary but may be added if desired.

3. Whole brown rice may be used instead of millet.

4. For extra nourishment one or two eggs may be added before putting the pudding in the oven, either with or without fruit. Eat hot or cold.

BAKED CUSTARD

Grain Free   Gluten Free

Imperial (Metric)	*American*
3 *free range eggs*	3 *free range eggs*
2 *teaspoons honey or raw cane sugar*	2 *teaspoons honey or raw cane sugar*
¾ *pint (425ml) milk*	2 *cups milk*
1 *bay leaf or grated nutmeg*	1 *bay leaf or grated nutmeg*
(optional)	*(optional)*

1. Beat eggs and honey very well in an ovenproof dish. Gradually add milk, beating all the time. Place bay leaf on the top or sprinkle a little grated nutmeg over.

2. Stand dish in a larger dish (eg. roasting pan) of cold water as custard must not boil.

3. Cook in a warm oven at 325°F/170°C (Gas Mark 3) for 45-60 minutes until set. Serve hot or cold, on its own or with fruit.

CARAMEL CUSTARD

Grain Free   Gluten Free

Use ½ pint (275ml, 1⅓ cups) milk, 2 eggs, less honey and mix in a basin as described above.

For Caramel:
Slowly heat 1 tablespoon honey in a saucepan until it changes colour. Coat sides of ovenproof dish with caramel and add well beaten mixture. Cook as above. Cool and carefully turn out on to a dish.

CUSTARD/MILK PUDDING

Grain Free   Gluten Free   Milk Free

Vary flours to suit individual needs and tastes, eg., brown rice flour may be used for a gluten free diet. For a full list of flours see page 00. Wholemeal (wholewheat) flour, goat's milk or cow's milk may also be used.

Custard:

Imperial (Metric)

1½ oz (40g) chickpea flour
½ oz (15g) soya flour
2 teaspoons raw cane sugar
1 pint (570ml) soya milk
2 free range egg yolks
a few drops of natural vanilla essence
  or a vanilla pod

American

2 tablespoons garbanzo flour
1 tablespoon soy flour
2 teaspoons raw cane sugar
2½ cups soy milk
2 free range egg yolks
a few drops of natural vanilla essence
  or a vanilla pod

1. Mix the flours and sugar with a little cold milk to a smooth paste.

2. Heat remainder of the milk (with vanilla pod if used) to nearly boiling.

3. Remove pod if used and pour on to blended flour, stirring all the time.

4. Return custard to saucepan and simmer for 5 minutes. Cool slightly before adding beaten egg yolks and vanilla essence.

Milk Pudding:

Prepare as for custard but omit egg yolks. Boil for 1 minute only and put into an oiled ovenproof dish. Cook in the oven at 325°F/170°C (Gas Mark 3) for 20-30 minutes.

Notes:

1. Sweet white sauce — make as for custard but omit eggs.

2. Ginger sauce — to sweet white sauce add 1 teaspoon ground ginger, a little lemon juice and raw cane sugar to taste.

3. Caramel sauce — make caramel by slowly heating 1 tablespoon honey in a saucepan until it changes colour. Stir into sweet white sauce.

4. Pink blancmange — to sweet white sauce add 2 teaspoons beetroot (beet) juice or hibiscus herb tea (see page 216).

CUSTARD SAUCE

Grain Free	Gluten Free

Imperial (Metric)	*American*
½ pint (285ml) milk	*1⅓ cups milk*
2 free range egg yolks	*2 free range egg yolks*
1 tablespoon raw cane sugar	*1 tablespoon raw cane sugar*
a few drops of natural vanilla essence, or a vanilla pod, or a few strips of lemon rind to flavour	*a few drops of natural vanilla essence, or a vanilla pod, or a few strips of lemon rind to flavor*

1. Warm milk and leave lemon rind or vanilla pod to infuse for 10 minutes, then remove. Bring milk to the boil, then allow to cool for 2-3 minutes. Add the beaten egg yolks and sugar, mixing well.

2. Reheat very gently until the custard thickens and coats the back of a spoon. Do not let the custard boil or it will curdle. If it begins to curdle, whisk briefly for 2-3 seconds. Add vanilla essence if not using the other methods of flavouring.

MAGIC CREAM

Grain Free   Gluten Free   Milk Free

Imperial (Metric)

1 free range egg, lightly poached
2 teaspoons clear honey
2-4 drops natural vanilla essence or
  lemon juice
2 tablespoons pure vegetable oil

American

1 free range egg, lightly poached
2 teaspoons clear honey
2-4 drops natural vanilla essence or
  lemon juice
2 tablespoons pure vegetable oil

1. Liquidize the first three ingredients together into a smooth cream. If too thick add a little water and blend in.

2. Add oil a little at a time, mixing well between each addition.

3. Keeps in 'fridge for up to 3 days.

TOFU WHIPPED CREAM

Grain Free   Gluten Free   Milk Free   Egg Free

Tofu, or soybean curd, is high in protein, low in fats, yet rich in polyunsaturates. You can buy it in most health shops. This makes a delicious cream.

Imperial (Metric)

1 10½ oz (297g) pack silken tofu
4 tablespoons safflower or sunflower
  oil
1 tablespoon honey
½ teaspoon lemon juice
1 teaspoon natural vanilla essence

American

1¼ cups silken tofu
4 tablespoons safflower or sunflower
  oil
1 tablespoon honey
½ teaspoon lemon juice
1 teaspoon natural vanilla essence

1. Whisk the ingredients together to make a thick cream.

2. Add puréed fruit of choice to this to make a delicious sweet.

NUT CREAM

Grain Free	Gluten Free	Milk Free	Egg Free

Put nuts of your choice in a liquidizer and add water, (bottled or filtered if necessary) to make a spreading consistency. Add more water to make a cream for topping fruit etc.

YOGURT ICE CREAM

Grain Free	Gluten Free	Egg Free

Imperial (Metric)

¼ pint (140ml) double cream
½ pint (285ml) homemade yogurt
honey or raw cane sugar to taste
½ lb (225g) puréed allowed fruit
such as:- pears, rhubarb, figs,
guavas, pineapple (chopped small),
mangoes or kiwi fruit or chopped
walnuts or hazelnuts

American

⅔ cup heavy cream
1⅓ cups homemade yogurt
honey or raw cane sugar to taste
2 cups puréed allowed fruit such as:-
pears, rhubarb, figs, guavas,
pineapple (chopped small),
mangoes or kiwi fruit or chopped
English walnuts or hazelnuts

1. Whip the cream until stiff, and then add to the yogurt.

2. Stir in honey or natural sugar to taste.

3. Mix all ingredients well, then freeze. Remove after 1 hour and remix with a fork. Replace for a final freeze.

Note: Kiwi fruit may cause reaction.

CAROB ICE CREAM

Grain Free	Gluten Free	Egg Free

Makes a soft ice cream.

Imperial (Metric)

1 large (14.5 oz/411g) tin evaporated milk, chilled
1 rounded tablespoon carob powder, sieved
4 tablespoons raw cane sugar
4 tablespoons water

American

1 large can evaporated milk, chilled
1 rounded tablespoon carob powder, sieved
4 tablespoons raw cane sugar
4 tablespoons water

1. Chill evaporated milk for 2 hours in a 'fridge or ½ hour in a freezer.

2. Mix carob powder, raw cane sugar and water.

3. Place evaporated milk in a fairly large bowl and beat until thick and nearly treble the quantity.

4. Fold in the carob mixture until well mixed.

5. Place in two plastic ice cream containers and freeze.

6. Remove from freezer about 10 minutes before serving.

Note: Replace the carob powder with 4 oz (115g) ground hazelnuts.

LEFT OVER CHRISTMAS PUDDING OR CAKE

Crumble mixture into a basin. Add a little beaten butter or margarine, sugar and lemon juice. Mix well and put on to squares of pastry. Top each one with another pastry square, dampen edges and seal to form an envelope shape. Bake at 400°F/200°C (Gas Mark 6) for approximately 35 minutes.

FRUIT LAYER

Put a layer of crushed semi-sweet biscuits, Ryvita or Prewett wheatflakes, etc. in an ovenproof dish. Add a layer of fruit (any safe fresh or dried fruits of choice) and a little raw cane sugar. Continue layers, finishing with biscuits. Pour over 1 cup of hot water and dot with butter or margarine.
Bake at 325°F/170°C (Gas Mark 4) for approximately 45 minutes.

PEAR AND MINCEMEAT PUDDING

Arrange 2 or 3 sliced ripe pears overlapping them in a greased sandwich tin. Sprinkle with a little sugar. Spread approximately 4-5 tablespoons mincemeat over pears.
Prepare a plain sponge topping with 2 eggs, 2 oz (55g, ¼ cup) butter or margarine, 2 oz (55g, ⅓ cup) sugar and 2 oz (55g, ½ cup) self-raising wholemeal (wholewheat) flour.
Bake at 350°F/180°C (Gas Mark 4) for approximately 35 minutes.

6.

BREADS AND CAKES

FLOUR

Some children may find wholemeal (wholewheat) flour too heavy. We suggest you try 81%-85% wheatmeal flours to start with and gradually mix these with wholemeal (wholewheat) flour so that the transition is not too drastic.

When sieving these flours the bran will be left behind. You can either add this to the sieved flour or sprinkle it over the bottom of the baking tin.

Few people realise that one third of the grain is removed in the milling of white flour, and that this is the part which contains vitamin E, the B vitamins, and essential minerals such as calcium, zinc, magnesium, manganese, copper and iron. The manufacturers are required by law to put back only four — vitamin B_1 (thiamine), vitamin B_3 (niacin), calcium in the form of chalk, and iron. The other important B vitamins (including vitamin B_6 (pyridoxine) and folic acid) vitamin E, the other minerals, and fibre are excluded.

White bread also has added to it chemical preservatives, bleaching agents, mould retardants, emulsifiers and improvers. Wholemeal (wholewheat) bread and some of the 81%-85% flours recommended, do not have these additives. Cheaper wholemeal (wholewheat) flours may be white flours which have been coloured. If in doubt, do not buy.

HOMEMADE WHOLEMEAL (WHOLEWHEAT) BREAD

Milk Free	Egg Free

Imperial (Metric)	*American*
1½ lb (680g) 100% *wholemeal flour*	1½ pounds 100% *wholewheat flour*
2 teaspoons sea salt	2 teaspoons sea salt
1 oz (30g) fresh yeast or ½ oz (15g) dried yeast	2½ tablespoons fresh yeast or 1 heaped tablespoon dried yeast
2 teaspoons honey	2 teaspoons honey
2 tablespoons safflower or sunflower oil	2 tablespoons safflower or sunflower oil
¾ pint (425ml) warm water	2 cups warm water

1. Put the flour and salt into a warmed bowl.

2. Put the warm water into another bowl, blend in the yeast and honey and leave until frothy.

3. Add this to the flour mixture, then mix in the oil. Mix well together, then tip on to a floured board, and knead for 2-3 minutes until it feels firm and elastic and no longer sticky.

4. Cover, and leave for half an hour in a warm place before dividing.

5. Divide into 2 or 3 pieces and put into oiled tins — more fun if the tins are all different, for instance you can buy animal shapes.

6. Cover with a clean tea towel, or greased polythene bag, and leave in a warm place until the dough has doubled in size.

7. Bake at 400°F/200°C (Gas Mark 6) for 10 minutes, then reduce the heat to 350°F/180°C (Gas Mark 4) for a further 25-35 minutes. If the bread is cooked it should sound hollow when tapped on the base with the knuckles.

8. When cooked, turn out onto a wire rack to cool.

YEAST FREE POTATO BREAD

Grain Free   Gluten Free   Milk Free

Imperial (Metric)

4 oz (115g) potato farina (flour)
2 heaped tablespoons soya flour
2 level teaspoons grain free baking
  powder
pinch sea salt
1 oz (30g) milk free margarine or 1
  tablespoon oil
1 teaspoon raw cane sugar
1 beaten free range egg
4 fl oz (120ml) water

American

¾ cup potato farina (flour)
2 heaped tablespoons soy flour
2 level teaspoons grain free baking
  powder
pinch sea salt
2½ tablespoons milk free margarine
  or 1 tablespoon oil
1 teaspoon raw cane sugar
1 beaten free range egg
½ cup water

1. Sieve together potato farina, soya (soy) flour, baking powder and salt. Rub in margarine or oil and then add sugar and stir.

2. Add beaten egg and water and whisk or beat to a smooth batter.

3. Put into a greased or oiled 1 lb (455g) lined loaf tin and bake at 400°F/200°C (Gas Mark 6) for about 35 minutes.

4. Turn out on to a wire rack to cool.

Note: A little soya (soy) bran could be added to this recipe to give dietary fibre.

Reproduced by kind permission of Foodwatch.

GLUTEN FREE BREAD

Gluten Free   Milk Free   Egg Free

Imperial (Metric)

4 *level teaspoons dried yeast*
1 *teaspoon raw cane sugar*
1 *Vitamin C tablet*
1 *pint (570ml) warm water*
1 *lb (455g) brown rice flour*
4 *oz (115g) soya flour*
pinch sea salt or salt substitute

American

4 *level teaspoons dried yeast*
1 *teaspoon raw cane sugar*
1 *Vitamin C tablet*
2½ *cups warm water*
3 *cups brown rice flour*
1 *cup soy flour*
pinch sea salt or salt substitute

1. Mix dried yeast, sugar and Vitamin C tablet with warm water. Leave to stand for 10-15 minutes.

2. Place flours and salt in a bowl and add yeast mixture, mixing well to make a thick batter consistency.

3. Divide between 3 1 lb (455g) oiled loaf tins and leave to rise in a warm place until doubled in size.

4. Bake in the oven at 400°F/200°C (Gas Mark 6) for approximately 30 minutes.

5. Cool slightly and remove from tins. Cover with a clean cloth to stop top becoming too crusty.

Note: Texture is quite different from ordinary bread and should not be compared. Flours vary from batch to batch and more water may be needed.

HERBED CHEESE BREAD

Imperial (Metric)

½ lb (225g) self-raising wholemeal
   flour
freshly ground pepper and sea salt
1 level teaspoon mustard powder
1 level tablespoon chopped fresh
   chives or 1 teaspoon dried herbs
1 level tablespoon chopped fresh
   parsley or 1 teaspoon dried
4 oz (115g) cheddar cheese, grated
1 oz (30g) unsalted butter or
   margarine
1 free range egg, beaten
¼ pint (140ml) water

American

2 cups self-raising wholewheat flour
freshly ground pepper and sea salt
1 level teaspoon mustard powder
1 level tablespoon chopped fresh
   chives or 1 teaspoon dried herbs
1 level tablespoon chopped fresh
   parsley or 1 teaspoon dried
1 cup cheddar cheese, grated
2½ tablespoons unsalted butter or
   margarine
1 free range egg, beaten
⅔ cup water

1. Grease a 1 lb (455g) loaf tin.

2. Mix the flour, salt, pepper, mustard, herbs and cheese together in a bowl.

3. Melt the butter and add to the flour with the egg and water. Mix well to form a soft dropping consistency.

4. Spoon into prepared tin and bake in the oven at 375°F/190°C (Gas Mark 5) for 45 minutes or until golden brown. Leave to cool on a wire rack. Serve sliced and buttered.

CHICKPEA (GARBANZO) AND RICE FLOUR CRISPBREADS

Gluten Free   Milk Free   Egg Free

Imperial (Metric)

2 oz (55g) fat (milk free)
4 oz (115g) chickpea flour
3 oz (85g) brown rice flour
pinch sea salt or salt substitute
water to mix

American

¼ cup fat (milk free)
¾ cup garbanzo flour
¾ cup less 1½ tablespoons brown
   rice flour
pinch sea salt or salt substitute
water to mix

1. Rub fat into flours and salt.

2. Add enough water (filtered or bottled if necessary) to make a firm dough.

3. Roll out to ⅛ inch (5mm) and cut into shapes. Place on an oiled baking sheet.

4. Bake at 350°F/180°C (Gas Mark 4) for 10-15 minutes or until golden brown.
Makes 24 crispbreads. Store in airtight tin or freeze.

Note: For Grain Free and Milk Free Crispbreads
The above basic recipe can be varied using flours and fat suitable to the individual and allergies concerned. For list of flours see page 235.

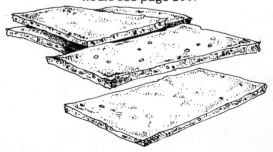

SHORTCRUST PASTRY

Egg Free

Imperial (Metric)	**American**
½ lb (225g) plain 100% wholemeal or 81%-85% wheatmeal flour	2 cups 100% wholewheat or 81%-85% wheatmeal flour
½ teaspoon sea salt	½ teaspoon sea salt
2 level teaspoons baking powder	2 level teaspoons baking powder
4 oz (115g) margarine or 2 oz (55g) margarine and 2 oz (55g) vegetable fat	½ cup margarine or ¼ cup margarine and ¼ cup vegetable fat
cold water to mix, about 2 tablespoons	cold water to mix, about 2 tablespoons

1. Sift together flour, salt and baking powder.

2. Rub in fat until mixture resembles fine breadcrumbs.

3. Add water. Roll out on floured board, taking care as wholemeal pastry is more crumbly than white flour pastry.

GLUTEN FREE PASTRY

Gluten Free

Imperial (Metric)	**American**
½ lb (225g) brown rice flour	1½ cups brown rice flour
1 oz (30g) soya flour	¼ cup soy flour
2 oz (55g) margarine	¼ cup margarine
2 oz (55g) vegetable fat	¼ cup vegetable fat
½ teaspoon gluten-free baking powder (optional)	½ teaspoon gluten-free baking powder (optional)
1 free range egg (approximately 40g)	1 free range egg (approximately 40g)
a little milk	a little milk

1. Place rice flour, soya (soy) flour, margarine, fat and baking powder into a bowl. Rub all together until mixture resembles breadcrumbs.

2. Add beaten egg and enough milk to form a soft dough. Roll out and bake at 435°F/225°C (Gas Mark 7) for 10-12 minutes (tarts) or 35-40 minutes (pies).

Note: Pastry can be pressed in dish in place of rolling, or used as a crumble.

GLUTEN FREE BISCUITS

Gluten Free

Imperial (Metric)	American
3 oz (85g) margarine	⅓ cup margarine
7 oz (200g) rice flour	1½ cups less 1½ tablespoons rice flour
1 oz (30g) soya flour	¼ cup soy flour
pinch sea salt	pinch sea salt
1 free range egg	1 free range egg
2½ oz (60g) raw cane sugar	⅓ cup + 1 tablespoon raw cane sugar

1. Either rub margarine into all dry ingredients together and bind with beaten egg, or cream fat and sugar together, add beaten egg and all other ingredients.

2. Roll out and cut into shapes. Place on an oiled baking sheet.

3. Bake at 350°F/180°C (Gas Mark 4) until golden brown. Two biscuits can be sandwiched together to make cream biscuits using butter cream or nut cream (see pages 139 and 175).

Note: Any of the following may be added to the above ingredients:-

1. 1 oz (30g, ⅓ cup) coconut.

2. 1 teaspoon ginger.

3. 1 tablespoon carob powder, sifted.

4. 2 oz (55g, ⅓ cup) dates or figs, finely chopped.

SESAME THINS

Egg Free

These are lovely served with soup or cheese, and you can vary the topping by using poppy or celery seeds.

Imperial (Metric)	**American**
½ lb (225g) plain wholemeal or 81%-85% wheatmeal flour	2 cups plain wholewheat or 81%-85% wheatmeal flour
2 oz (55g) maize flour	3 tablespoons cornmeal
1 level tablespoon raw cane sugar	1 level tablespoon raw cane sugar
½ level teaspoon bicarbonate of soda	½ level teaspoon baking soda
½ level teaspoon sea salt	½ level teaspoon sea salt
2 oz (55g) margarine	¼ cup margarine
5-6 tablespoons water	5-6 tablespoons water
1 tablespoon white vinegar	1 tablespoon white vinegar

Topping:

Imperial (Metric)	**American**
4 tablespoons sesame or sunflower seeds	4 tablespoons sesame or sunflower seeds
oil for coating	oil for coating

1. Put the flours, sugar, bicarbonate of soda (baking soda) and salt into a basin.

2. Rub in the margarine until it resembles fine breadcrumbs.

3. Add the water and vinegar, mix to a sconelike dough, then roll out until it is very thin.

4. Cut out with a circular biscuit cutter 2 inches (5cm) in diameter. Put biscuits on to a greased tray, then brush them with oil. Sprinkle them with sesame seeds, pressing the seeds on to the dough with the back of a spoon.

5. Bake in a moderate oven at 375°F/190°C (Gas Mark 5) for 10-15 minutes or until golden brown. Cool on a rack and store in an airtight tin.

YOGURT SCONES

Egg Free

Imperial (Metric)

½ lb (225g) wholemeal flour
1 level teaspoon bicarbonate of soda
   and 1 level teaspoon cream of
   tartar (or 2-3 teaspoons baking
   powder)
½ teaspoon sea salt
2 oz (55g) margarine
¼ pint (140ml) natural cow's or
   goat's yogurt

American

2 cups wholewheat flour
1 level teaspoon baking soda and 1
   level teaspoon cream of tartar (or
   2-3 teaspoons baking powder)
½ teaspoon sea salt
¼ cup margarine
⅔ cup plain cow's or goat's yogurt

1. Sift together the dry ingredients.

2. Rub in the margarine, then add the yogurt quickly, mixing with a knife to make a soft dough.

3. Roll out to about ½ inch (1cm) thickness. Cut with 1½ inch (3.5cm) diameter cutter.

4. Bake in a hot oven at 450°F/230°C (Gas Mark 8) for 10-12 minutes. Makes 12 scones. Best eaten fresh, but can be frozen.

HAZELNUT STREUSEL LOAF

Streusel:

Imperial (Metric)

4 oz (115g) hazelnuts, chopped
3 oz (85g) raw cane sugar
1 oz (30g) butter, melted
½ teaspoon cinnamon

American

¾ cup hazelnuts, chopped
½ cup raw cane sugar
2½ tablespoons butter, melted
½ teaspoon cinnamon

Loaf:

Imperial (Metric)

2 oz (55g) butter or margarine
½ lb (225g) 81%-85% wheatmeal flour
3 oz (85g) dates or figs, chopped
2 free range eggs
2 tablespoons honey
¼ pint (140ml) milk

American

¼ cup butter or margarine
2 cups 81%-85% wheatmeal flour
½ cup dates or figs, chopped
2 free range eggs
2 tablespoons honey
⅔ cup milk

1. Mix the ingredients for the streusel together.

2. Make the loaf by rubbing the butter into the flour and adding the chopped fruit. Mix the eggs, honey and milk and pour over the flour mixture, mixing well.

3. Oil and line a 2 lb (900g) loaf tin and pour half the mixture into it. Sprinkle over half the streusel. Cover with the rest of the loaf mixture, then the remaining streusel. Bake at 350°F/180°C (Gas Mark 4) for 1 hour.

Note: Can be served as a pudding with a custard.

PEAR CAKE

This is a good way of using up overripe pears.

Imperial (Metric)	American
1 lb (455g) ripe pears	1 pound ripe pears
1 lb (455g) 100% wholemeal flour	1 pound 100% wholewheat flour
3 teaspoons baking powder	3 teaspoons baking powder
5 oz (140g) margarine	½ cup + 2½ tablespoons margarine
4 oz (115g) muscovado sugar	⅔ cup muscovado sugar
2 teaspoons cinnamon	2 teaspoons cinnamon
2 large free range eggs	2 large free range eggs

Topping:

Imperial (Metric)	American
2 tablespoons ground hazelnuts	2 tablespoons ground hazelnuts
2 tablespoons desiccated coconut	2 tablespoons desiccated coconut
1 tablespoon muscovado sugar	1 tablespoon muscovado sugar

1. Liquidize the pears.

2. Sift together the flour and baking powder. Rub the fat into the flour.

3. Add the sugar and cinnamon. Then mix in the eggs and pears, stirring well.

4. Put into a greased 7 inch (18cm) square cake tin.

5. Mix the topping ingredients together and sprinkle on to the cake mixture. Bake at 350°F/180°C (Gas Mark 4) for 1 hour.

BASIC SPONGE/PUDDING RECIPE

Gluten Free   Milk Free

For a grain free recipe substitute potato flour or other grain free flour of choice for rice flour.

Imperial (Metric)

6 oz (170g) milk free margarine
4 oz (115g) raw cane sugar, vanilla flavoured
3 free range eggs
3 oz (85g) brown rice flour
3 oz (85g) chickpea or split pea flour
1 oz (30g) soya flour
3 heaped teaspoons grain free baking powder
a little water

American

⅔ cup milk free margarine
⅔ cup raw cane sugar, vanilla flavoured
3 free range eggs
¾ cup less 1½ tablespoons brown rice flour
¾ cup less 1½ tablespoons garbanzo or split pea flour
¼ cup soy flour
3 heaped teaspoons grain free baking powder
a little water

1. Oil two 8 inch (20cm) round cake tins.

2. Cream margarine and sugar until light and fluffy. Add beaten eggs, slowly, one at a time. Stir sifted flours and baking powder together and fold into mixture. Add water if necessary to make a dropping consistency.

3. Bake at 350°F/180°C (Gas Mark 4) for approximately 20 minutes. Will also make 32 small cakes.

Note: Variations:

1. Add 2 oz (55g, ½ cup) carob powder, sieved.

2. Add 2-3 oz (55-85g, ½-⅔ cup) chopped nuts or peel.

3. Filling: Use marzipan paste recipe on page 171.

4. Makes a delicious, good size sponge pudding. Use a 2 pint (1 litre) basin.

5. Cream cakes: Make 32 small cakes with basic mixture, and bake for 10-15 minutes. Cool, cut off the tops and fill with any 'safe' filling of choice.

CINNAMON AND GINGER CAKE WITH STICKY LEMON TOPPING

Gluten Free

Imperial (Metric)	American
½ lb (225g) brown rice flour	1½ cups brown rice flour
3 teaspoons grain free baking powder	3 teaspoons grain free baking powder
4 oz (115g) margarine	½ cup margarine
1 tablespoon muscovado sugar	1 tablespoon muscovado sugar
2 teaspoons ground ginger	2 teaspoons ground ginger
1 teaspoon ground cinnamon	1 teaspoon ground cinnamon
3 tablespoons black treacle or molasses	3 tablespoons molasses
2 tablespoons hot water	2 tablespoons hot water
1 free range egg	1 free range egg

1. Sieve together flour and baking powder. Rub the fat into the flour. Add the other ingredients and mix well.

2. Put into an oiled 6 inch (15cm) tin, and bake in a moderate oven at 350°F/180°C (Gas Mark 4) for 1 hour.

For lemon topping:

Imperial (Metric)	American
4 oz (115g) muscovado sugar	⅔ cup muscovado sugar
2 tablespoons lemon juice	2 tablespoons lemon juice

1. Mix the sugar and lemon juice and pour over the top of the warm cake. Leave until cold, then lift from the tin.

QUICK LEMON BUNS

Makes 24

Imperial (Metric)

2 oz (55g) wholemeal self-raising
    flour
4 oz (115g) wheatmeal self-raising
    flour
4 oz (115g) margarine, softened
3 oz (85g) raw cane sugar
2 free range eggs
grated rind of 1 lemon
1 teaspoon baking powder
4 tablespoons milk

American

½ cup wholewheat self-raising flour
1 cup wheatmeal self-raising flour
½ cup margarine, softened
½ cup raw cane sugar
2 free range eggs
grated rind of 1 lemon
1 teaspoon baking powder
4 tablespoons milk

Topping:

Imperial (Metric)

1 teaspoon honey
a little lemon juice
desiccated coconut

American

1 teaspoon honey
a little lemon juice
desiccated coconut

1. Sift flours and baking powder, put all cake ingredients into a bowl and mix well.

2. Have bun tins ready with 24 baking cases standing inside them, and spoon mixture equally into them.

3. Bake in a preheated oven at 375°F/190°C (Gas Mark 5) for approximately 20 minutes.

4. To make the topping, mix the honey with a little lemon juice to make a thin liquid. Spread over cooled buns to give glaze effect, and sprinkle with desiccated coconut.

Note: Substitute the topping with No-Sugar Icing (page 173).

QUICK CAROB BUNS

Imperial (Metric)	American
4 oz (115g) margarine	*½ cup margarine*
½ lb (225g) 81%-85% wheatmeal self-raising flour or plain wholemeal flour with ½ teaspoon baking powder	*2 cups 81%-85% wheatmeal self-raising flour or plain wholewheat flour with ½ teaspoon baking powder*
3 oz (85g) raw cane sugar	*½ cup raw cane sugar*
2 oz (55g) carob powder	*½ cup carob powder*
1 free range egg	*1 free range egg*
allowed jam or honey	*allowed jam or honey*
a little milk for glaze	*a little milk for glaze*

1. Rub the margarine into the flour. Add the sugar and carob. Beat the egg and add to the mixture to make a stiff paste.

2. Put the mixture into bun tins, make a hole in the middle of each bun, and put in about ½ teaspoon of allowed honey or jam. Draw mixture over the top of jam or honey and seal.

3. Brush with milk and bake for 15 minutes at 375°F/190°C (Gas Mark 5).

Note: You can replace the carob powder with 2 oz (55g, ⅓ cup) chopped dates or figs, or 2 oz (55g, ⅔ cup) coconut.

CAROB BARS

Makes 10

Egg Free

Imperial (Metric)

4 oz (115g) margarine or butter
1 oz (30g) raw cane sugar
4 oz (115g) wholemeal self-raising
  flour
1 oz (30g) desiccated coconut
1 oz (30g) ground brown rice flour

American

½ cup margarine or butter
2 tablespoons raw cane sugar
1 cup wholewheat self-raising flour
⅓ cup desiccated coconut
1½ tablespoons ground brown rice
  flour

Carob Icing:

Imperial (Metric)

1 oz (30g) butter
1 tablespoon honey
2 level tablespoons carob powder,
  sieved

American

2½ tablespoons butter
1 tablespoon honey
2 level tablespoons carob powder,
  sieved

1. Line a small loaf tin with oiled greaseproof paper. Cream margarine and sugar until fluffy. Work in dry ingredients.

2. Spread mixture evenly in the tin and bake at 350°F/180°C (Gas Mark 4) for approximately 20 minutes or until golden brown.

3. To make Carob Icing, gently heat butter and honey until melted. Do not allow to boil. Add carob powder and blend well. Spread over warm biscuit mixture.

4. Leave to set. Cut into 10 squares and put into paper cases.

COCONUT PYRAMIDS

Makes 12

Grain Free   **Gluten Free**   **Milk Free**

For grain free recipe omit rice paper.

Imperial (Metric)

4 oz (115g) desiccated coconut
2 tablespoons honey or ground
   demerara sugar
2 free range egg whites

American

1⅓ cups desiccated coconut
2 tablespoons honey or ground
   demerara sugar
2 free range egg whites

1. Combine the above ingredients. The mixture should be stiff enough to make into pyramid shapes. Add a little more coconut if needed.

2. Use 1 tablespoon of mixture to make each shape.

3. Put shapes into oiled bun cases or on to rice paper, and bake in a slow oven at 300°F/150°C (Gas Mark 2) for approximately 20 minutes.

HAZELNUT MACAROONS

Makes 12

Grain Free   Gluten Free   Milk Free

Imperial (Metric)

4 oz (115g) ground hazelnuts
3 oz (85g) ground raw cane sugar
2 small free range egg whites
whole hazelnuts to decorate

American

¾ cup ground hazelnuts
½ cup ground raw cane sugar
2 small free range egg whites
whole hazelnuts to decorate

1. Mix the above ingredients except the whole nuts. If you like a crispy top, save some egg white to brush the tops.

2. Oil and flour a baking tray, shaking off excess flour, or line with rice paper.

3. Put teaspoons of mixture on to the tray, and place a whole hazelnut in the middle of each.

4. Bake in a moderate oven at 350°F/180°C (Gas Mark 4) for 15-20 minutes.

Note: You can vary the mixture by using 3 oz (85g, ⅔ cup) hazelnuts, and 1 oz (30g, 3 tablespoons) brazil or walnuts.

COCONUT BARS

Makes about 15 bars

Pastry:

Imperial (Metric)

6 oz (170g) 81%-85% wheatmeal flour
4 oz (115g) margarine or unsalted butter
2 oz (55g) raw cane sugar

American

1½ cups 81%-85% wheatmeal flour
½ cup margarine or unsalted butter
⅓ cup raw cane sugar

1. Put flour, margarine, and sugar into a bowl and mix into a dough.

2. Press mixture into an oiled medium-sized Swiss roll tin and bake in the oven at 350°F/180°C (Gas Mark 4) for approximately 20 minutes.

Topping:

Imperial (Metric)	American
2 free range egg whites	2 free range egg whites
2 oz (55g) raw cane sugar	⅓ cup raw cane sugar
4 oz (115g) desiccated coconut	1⅓ cups desiccated coconut
allowed jam	allowed jam

3. Whisk egg whites until stiff, and add remaining ingredients. Spread a little 'safe' jam if desired evenly on top of pastry mixture, then cover with the coconut topping.

4. Return to the oven for a further 25-30 minutes, or until top is golden brown. Cool in the tin and cut into slices when cold.

Note: Replace the coconut with chopped walnuts or hazelnuts.

FLAPJACKS

Egg Free

Imperial (Metric)	American
5 oz (140g) margarine	½ cup + 2½ tablespoons margarine
3 oz (85g) raw cane sugar	½ cup raw cane sugar
1 tablespoon molasses or black treacle	1 tablespoon molasses
½ lb (225g) rolled oats	2 cups rolled oats

1. Melt margarine, sugar and molasses slowly in a large saucepan and add oats.

2. Spread into an oiled shallow 6 inch (15cm) square baking tin and bake at 375°F/190°C (Gas Mark 5) for approximately 20-25 minutes.

3. Mark into squares while still hot, and remove from tin when cold. For special occasions put into cake cases. Makes 20.

OAT CRUNCHIES

Makes 24

Egg Free

Imperial (Metric)

4 oz (115g) margarine
3 oz (85g) raw cane sugar
1 teaspoon honey
1 teaspoon bicarbonate of soda,
  stirred into a teaspoon boiling
  water
4 oz (115g) oats
4 oz (115g) 85% wheatmeal self-
  raising flour

American

½ cup margarine
½ cup raw cane sugar
1 teaspoon honey
1 teaspoon baking soda, stirred into a
  teaspoon boiling water
1 cup oats
1 cup 85% wheatmeal self-raising
  flour

1. Melt the margarine, sugar, honey and bicarbonate of soda (baking soda) in a pan. Stir in the oats and flour and mix well.

2. Place teaspoons of the mixture on to a greased baking sheet.

3. Bake at 350°F/180°C (Gas Mark 4) for 20 minutes. These are quick and easy to make and are delicious.

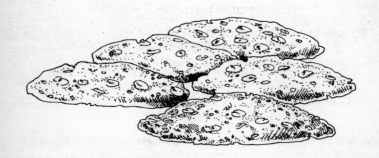

CRUNCHIE COOKIES

Makes 24

Milk Free   Egg Free

Imperial (Metric)

4 oz (115g) wholemeal self-raising
  flour
2 oz (55g) rolled oats
2-3 oz (55-85g) raw cane sugar
1 oz (30g) desiccated coconut
4 oz (115g) crunchy peanut butter
grated rind of 1 lemon
½ teaspoon ground cinnamon or
  ginger
¼ teaspoon bicarbonate of soda
1 tablespoon clear honey
2 fl oz (60ml) water

American

1 cup wholewheat self-raising flour
½ cup rolled oats
⅓-½ cup raw cane sugar
⅓ cup desiccated coconut
1 cup crunchy peanut butter
grated rind of 1 lemon
½ teaspoon ground cinnamon or
  ginger
¼ teaspoon baking soda
1 tablespoon clear honey
¼ cup water

1. Lightly oil two baking sheets.

2. Place sifted flour, all dry ingredients and peanut butter in a
    bowl and mix well.

3. Warm honey and water in a pan and add to the mixture.

4. Shape into small balls approximately 1 inch (2cm) in
diameter and place on the baking sheets. Flatten with a fork,
    making a cross pattern on the cookie.

5. Bake in a preheated oven at 350°F/180°C (Gas Mark 4) for
    15-20 minutes.

Note: Leave the cookies as balls, and call them footballs or
    cannon balls. They look good in petit four cases.

CANNON BALLS

Makes 14

Milk Free   Egg Free

Imperial (Metric)

4 oz (115g) wholemeal self-raising
  flour
1 level teaspoon ground ginger
1 level teaspoon ground cinnamon
½ level teaspoon ground fennel
½ level teaspoon ground nutmeg
3 tablespoons safflower or sunflower
  oil
2 tablespoons molasses

American

1 cup wholewheat self-raising flour
1 level teaspoon ground ginger
1 level teaspoon ground cinnamon
½ level teaspoon ground fennel
½ level teaspoon ground nutmeg
3 tablespoons safflower or sunflower
  oil
2 tablespoons molasses

1. Blend flour and spices in a mixing bowl. Warm oil and molasses in a pan and mix all together.

2. Add a little water to make a stiff dough.

3. Break off one inch (2cm) diameter pieces, and roll into 12-14 balls.

4. Bake on a lightly oiled and floured baking tray at 375°F/190°C (Gas Mark 5) for 12 minutes.

LEMON SHORTBREAD

Egg Free

Imperial (Metric)

4 oz (115g) butter
3 oz (85g) raw cane sugar
2 teaspoons lemon juice
grated rind of ½ lemon
4 oz (115g) wholemeal flour
2 oz (55g) brown rice flour

American

½ cup butter
½ cup raw cane sugar
2 teaspoons lemon juice
grated rind of ½ lemon
1 cup wholewheat flour
3 tablespoons brown rice flour

1. Cream together softened butter and sugar. Add juice and rind of lemon, then the flour and ground rice. Rub the mixture together with your fingers until it forms a shortbread dough.

2. Roll it out and cut into fingers. Crimp the ends of the fingers and prick with a fork.

3. Put into a greased baking tin and bake for 30 minutes at 325°F/170°C (Gas Mark 3). Cool and store in an airtight tin.

CELEBRATION SHORTBREAD

Egg Free

Imperial (Metric)	American
5 oz (140g) butter	½ cup + 2½ tablespoons butter
3 oz (85g) raw cane sugar	½ cup raw cane sugar
grated rind of 1 lemon	grated rind of 1 lemon
2 oz (55g) crystallized ginger, chopped fine	⅓ cup crystallized ginger, chopped fine
1 oz (30g) cut lemon peel	1 heaped tablespoon cut lemon peel
4 oz (115g) wholemeal flour	1 cup wholewheat flour
4 oz (115g) brown rice flour	¾ cup brown rice flour
1 oz (30g) chopped hazelnuts	¼ cup chopped hazelnuts

1. Cream the butter until soft then add the remaining ingredients, except the hazelnuts. Work the mixture together to make a dough.

2. Press into a greased 8 inch (20cm) round cake tin. Crimp the edges and prick all over with a fork. Mark into 8 pieces, and top with chopped hazelnuts.

3. Bake in the centre of the oven at 350°F/180°C (Gas Mark 4) for 45 minutes until the hazelnuts are golden brown. Remove from tin when cold. This shortbread keeps well in a tin for up to 2 weeks.

GINGERBREAD MEN

Egg Free

Imperial (Metric)	**American**
4 oz (115g) margarine	½ cup margarine
½ lb (225g) 81%-85% wheatmeal flour	2 cups 81%-85% wheatmeal flour
3 oz (85g) demerara or muscovado sugar	½ cup demerara or muscovado sugar
2 tablespoons black treacle (or molasses)	2 tablespoons black treacle (or molasses)
1 teaspoon ginger	1 teaspoon ginger
2 teaspoons lemon juice	2 teaspoons lemon juice
pieces of date or nuts for decoration	pieces of date or nuts for decoration

1. Rub the margarine into the flour. Add the sugar, treacle or molasses, ginger and juice to make a firm dough.

2. Roll out on a floured board and cut into shapes. If you do not have a gingerbread man shape, cut out a cardboard shape first, place it on the dough and cut around it. Use an egg slice to put the men on a floured baking sheet, and add pieces of date for eyes, nose, mouth and buttons.

3. Bake at 350°F/180°C (Gas Mark 4) for about 10-15 minutes. Cool on tray.

Note: You can also use this recipe to make ginger biscuits.

A MAYPOLE CAKE

1. Make two large circular sponge sandwich cakes with the Birthday Cake recipe (page 167) or the Basic Sponge/Pudding recipe (see page 154). Ice the top.

2. Find some thick wool in five different colours and cut a 20 inch (50cm) length of each. Hold the ends even and tie a loose loop in the centre. Slip this round a 10 inch (25cm) knitting needle, and pull tight.

3. Push the knitting needle into the centre of the cake. Separate the strands of wool and put them evenly round the edge of the cake, keeping them in place by pressing a walnut firmly into the icing.

BIRTHDAY CAKE

Imperial (Metric)	American
6 oz (170g) margarine	⅔ cup margarine
6 oz (170g) ground demerara sugar	1 cup ground demerara sugar
3 free range eggs	3 free range eggs
4 oz (115g) 81%-85% wheatmeal self-raising flour	1 cup 81%-85% wheatmeal self-raising flour
2 oz (55g) rice flour	3 tablespoons rice flour

1. Cream the margarine and sugar, add the eggs gradually, adding a tablespoon of flour if the mixture looks as though it might curdle. Using a metal spoon, fold in the mixed sifted self-raising flour and rice flour.

2. Bake in an oiled 7-8 inch (18-20cm) tin at 375°F/190°C (Gas Mark 5) for 40 minutes until a knife put into it comes out clean. Cool on a wire rack.

3. Cover with Fudge Icing (see page 173).

Note: You can cut the cake into the desired shape e.g. child's age or initials, and display on an upturned baking tray covered with foil. Decoration: Grated carob bar or carob chips, chopped hazelnuts or walnuts (English walnuts), desiccated coconut can be used to coat the sides of the cake. Off cuts from the cake can be cut into small shapes and decorated with icing, nuts, grated carob bar etc., and served in small paper cases at the party.

WHOLEMEAL HOT CROSS BUNS

Imperial (Metric)

1 oz (30g) fresh yeast or 1 level
tablespoon dried yeast plus 1
teaspoon demerara or molasses
sugar
½ pint (285ml) warm milk and
water mixed
1 lb (455g) 100% wholemeal flour
½ level teaspoon sea salt
1 level teaspoon ground cinnamon
½ level teaspoon ground nutmeg
2 oz (55g) demerara sugar
1 free range egg
2 oz (55g) margarine or unsalted
butter, melted
4 oz (115g) chopped dates or figs or
both
2 oz (55g) chopped crystallized
lemon peel

American

2½ tablespoons fresh yeast or 1 level
tablespoon dried yeast plus
1 teaspoon demerara or molasses
sugar
1⅓ cups warm milk and water mixed
4 cups 100% wholewheat flour
½ level teaspoon sea salt
1 level teaspoon ground cinnamon
½ level teaspoon ground nutmeg
⅓ cup demerara sugar
1 free range egg
¼ cup margarine or unsalted butter,
melted
⅔ cup chopped dates or figs or both
⅓ cup chopped crystallized lemon
peel

Glaze:

Imperial (Metric)

1 tablespoon milk
1 tablespoon demerara sugar, boiled
together until the sugar is dissolved

American

1 tablespoon milk
1 tablespoon demerara sugar, boiled
together until the sugar is dissolved

1. Stir fresh yeast into warmed milk and water. For dried yeast
stir sugar into milk mixture and sprinkle on dried yeast, leaving
for 10 minutes until frothy.

2. Mix flour, salt, spices and sugar in a warmed mixing bowl.
When the yeast is frothy add this to the flour with the egg.

melted butter, fruit and peel. Mix well, then leave covered with a cloth in a warm place until doubled in size.

3. When risen turn on to a floured board and divide into 12 equal portions.

4. Put on to greased baking tins and leave in a warm place until risen.

5. Make rice paper or pastry crosses and put on the buns.

6. Bake in the centre of a hot oven at 425°F/220°C (Gas Mark 7) for 15-20 minutes.

7. Brush the glaze over the buns while they are hot.

Note: Crystallized lemon peel is obtainable from health food stores or make your own (see below).

CITRUS PEEL FOR CAKES AND PUDDINGS

Grain Free	Gluten Free	Milk Free	Egg Free

Imperial (Metric)

4 tablespoons lemon or grapefruit peel, chopped into small pieces
1 pint (570ml) water
1 tablespoon sea salt

American

1 cup lemon or grapefruit peel, chopped into small pieces
2½ cups water
1 tablespoon sea salt

1. Use undyed fruit if possible. Scrub the skins well.

2. Mix the water and salt and soak the peel in it overnight.

3. Drain and rinse in clear water.

4. Use in rock cakes, fruit cakes, etc. Keeps in the 'fridge for several weeks.

BURY SIMNEL CAKE

Bury in Lancashire is famous for its simnels, where they are very popular on Mothering Sunday or Simnel Sunday. This is based on a traditional recipe which is not too rich and is easy to make.

Imperial (Metric)

2½ fl oz (75ml) milk
1 large free range egg
1 oz (30g) raw cane sugar
1 large tablespoon clear honey
½ lb (225g) wholemeal plain flour
2 teaspoons baking powder
1 level teaspoon cinnamon
¼ level teaspoon nutmeg
¼ level teaspoon ground fennel (optional)
1½ oz (45g) soft margarine or butter
5 oz (140g) dates, cut into small pieces
2 oz (55g) figs or soft dried pears, cut into small pieces
1 oz (30g) crystallized lemon or grapefruit peel (optional)
brazil nuts for decoration

American

¼ cup + 1 tablespoon milk
1 large free range egg
2 tablespoons raw cane sugar
1 large tablespoon clear honey
2 cups wholewheat plain flour
2 teaspoons baking powder
1 level teaspoon cinnamon
¼ level teaspoon nutmeg
¼ level teaspoon ground fennel (optional)
3¼ tablespoons soft margarine or butter
1 cup dates, cut into small pieces
⅓ cup figs or soft dried pears, cut into small pieces
1 heaped tablespoon crystallized lemon or grapefruit peel (optional)
brazil nuts for decoration

Marzipan:

Imperial (Metric)

1 oz (30g) ground hazelnuts
2 oz (55g) ground demerara sugar, vanilla flavoured, or add a few drops of natural vanilla essence
a little egg white

American

3 tablespoons ground hazelnuts
⅓ cup ground demerara sugar, vanilla flavoured, or add a few drops of natural vanilla essence
a little egg white

1. Mix the milk, egg, sugar and honey in a bowl.

2. In another basin sift the flour, baking powder, and spices, then rub in the margarine.

3. Add the fruit to the flour mixture, then the liquid, making a scone type soft dough. Flatten into a large circle on a lightly floured board.

4. Mix the marzipan ingredients with a wooden spoon to a firm paste. Place marzipan in a ball in the middle of the dough. Draw the dough up around the marzipan and seal. Flatten the ball into a round about 5 inches (13cm) across. Brush with remaining egg white and make a cross on top with brazil nuts.

5. Bake at 425°F/220°C (Gas Mark 7) for 40-45 minutes.

MARZIPAN

Grain Free   Gluten Free   Milk Free

Imperial (Metric)	American
4 oz (115g) cashews, hazelnuts or brazil nuts, ground	¾ cup cashews, hazelnuts or brazil nuts, ground
1 tablespoon clear honey	1 tablespoon clear honey
1 free range egg yolk	1 free range egg yolk
½ teaspoon natural vanilla essence	½ teaspoon natural vanilla essence

1. Mix all ingredients well together. This amount will cover an 8 inch (20cm) cake.

Notes:

1. For egg free marzipan omit the egg yolk.

2. Can also be used as a cake filling.

CHRISTMAS CAKE

Makes an 8 inch (20cm) cake

Imperial (Metric)

6 oz (170g) margarine or butter,
  softened
6 oz (170g) raw cane sugar
1 oz (30g) hazelnuts, ground
4 free range eggs
½ lb (225g) wholemeal or
  wheatmeal flour
1 level teaspoon cinnamon
1 level teaspoon nutmeg
½ level teaspoon fennel
pinch sea salt
¾ lb (340g) dried pears, chopped
  (remove any hard core)
¾ lb (340g) dates, chopped
6 oz (170g) dried bananas or figs,
  chopped
1 oz (30g) hazelnuts, chopped

American

⅔ cup margarine or butter, softened
1 cup raw cane sugar
¼ cup hazelnuts, ground
4 free range eggs
2 cups wholewheat or wheatmeal
  flour
1 level teaspoon cinnamon
1 level teaspoon nutmeg
½ level teaspoon fennel
pinch sea salt
2 cups dried pears, chopped (remove
  any hard core)
2 cups dates, chopped
1 cup dried bananas or figs, chopped
3 tablespoons hazelnuts, chopped

1. Line and oil an 8 inch (20cm) cake tin.

2. Beat margarine, sugar and ground hazelnuts until light and fluffy. Add eggs one at a time, beating well between each addition.

3. Sieve and fold in the flour, spices and salt. Add fruit and nuts. Mix carefully and thoroughly. Turn mixture into tin and smooth top with a palette-knife, leaving a slight hollow in the centre to allow for even rising.

4. Bake at 350°F/180°C (Gas Mark 4) for 2 hours. Cover top of cake with greaseproof paper for the last 30 minutes of cooking to prevent burning.

Notes: For a glaze — Gently heat a little 'safe' marmalade. Add a little water if necessary and sieve. Spread thinly over cake. Decorate with marzipan and icing (see page 171 and below). Dried fruit can be obtained from most health food stores.

NO-SUGAR ICING

Covers an 8 inch (20cm) cake or 24 small cakes

Grain Free	Gluten Free	Milk Free	Egg Free

Imperial (Metric)   **American**

4 oz (115g) coconut cream   1 cup coconut cream
2 tablespoons boiling water   2 tablespoons boiling water

1. Grate coconut cream, add boiling water and stir until creamy. Smooth over cake with a knife dipped in hot water and leave to set.

Note: For carob icing, add 2 tablespoons carob powder. Add water as necessary.

FUDGE ICING

Grain Free	Gluten Free	Egg Free

Imperial (Metric)   **American**

2 oz (55g) unsalted butter   ¼ cup unsalted butter
3 tablespoons milk   3 tablespoons milk
4 oz (115g) ground demerara sugar   ⅔ cup ground demerara sugar

1. Combine all the ingredients in a saucepan, and boil gently for ½ minute. Remove from heat and leave to cool. Beat well until thick.

2. Spread over the top of the cake, or slice cake horizontally and sandwich together with the icing.

WHITE CHRISTMAS CAKE

Imperial (Metric)	American
½ lb (225g) margarine or butter	1 cup margarine or butter
½ lb (225g) muscovado sugar	1⅓ cups muscovado sugar
4 large free range eggs	4 large free range eggs
¾ lb (340g) plain 81%-85% wheatmeal flour	3 cups plain 81%-85% wheatmeal flour
pinch sea salt	pinch sea salt
1 level teaspoon baking powder	1 level teaspoon baking powder
6 oz (170g) crystallized pineapple, chopped	1 cup crystallized pineapple, chopped
4 oz (115g) walnuts or hazelnuts, chopped	¾ cup English walnuts or hazelnuts, chopped
4 oz (115g) crystallized lemon peel, chopped (see page 169)	⅔ cup crystallized lemon peel, chopped (see page 169)
6 oz (170g) stem ginger, drained and chopped (optional)	1 cup stem ginger, drained and chopped (optional)
4 oz (115g) dates, chopped	⅔ cup dates, chopped
4 oz (115g) figs, chopped	⅔ cup figs, chopped
grated rind of 1 lemon	grated rind of 1 lemon
juice of ½ lemon	juice of ½ lemon

1. Cream margarine and sugar until light and fluffy. Beat in eggs gradually, adding a tablespoon of flour if mixture seems likely to curdle.

2. Sieve together flour, salt and baking powder, and fold into creamed mixture. Add remaining ingredients and juice. Mix gently. Put into a greased 8 inch (20cm) round cake tin.

3. Bake in a moderate oven at 325°F/170°C (Gas Mark 3) for 2½-3 hours, covering with greaseproof paper if necessary for the last hour to prevent burning.

Note: Crystallized pineapple and lemon peel are obtainable from health food stores.

BUTTER CREAM FILLING OR TOPPING

Grain Free	Gluten Free	Egg Free

For a milk free recipe use a milk free margarine, and soya (soy) milk for the topping.

Filling:

Imperial (Metric)	**American**
4 oz (115g) margarine	½ cup margarine
2 teaspoons ground raw cane sugar	2 teaspoons ground raw cane sugar
1 teaspoon hot water	1 teaspoon hot water
few drops of natural vanilla essence or oil	few drops of natural vanilla essence or oil

1. Cream margarine and sugar until light and fluffy. Whisk in the water and add vanilla essence to taste.

Topping: For a stiffer cream add a little dried milk powder (soya [soy], goat's, etc. as required) until desired consistency is reached.

Note: For pink or red cream, add a little beetroot juice, or for a carob filling add 2 oz (55g) carob powder, sieved, with extra hot water as required.

CAROB YOGURT FILLING

Grain Free	Gluten Free	Egg Free

Imperial (Metric)	**American**
¼ pint (140ml) thick set natural yogurt, or Greek yogurt	⅔ cup thick set plain yogurt
1 tablespoon carob powder, sieved	1 tablespoon carob powder, sieved
1 tablespoon clear honey	1 tablespoon clear honey

1. Combine all the ingredients together and use to sandwich a carob cake. Remember the yogurt will not keep long out of the 'fridge, so the cake needs to be eaten quickly.

CHRISTMAS PUDDING

Makes 2 1½ lb (675g)

Milk Free

Imperial (Metric)

2 oz (55g) wholemeal self-raising flour
½ level teaspoon ground cinnamon
½ level teaspoon ground nutmeg
¼ level teaspoon ground fennel
¼ level teaspoon sea salt
6 oz (170g) dates or figs, finely chopped
6 oz (170g) dried pears, finely chopped (remove any hard core)
3 oz (85g) crystallized lemon peel and/or pineapple, finely chopped (see page 169)
3 oz (85g) raw cane sugar
4 oz (115g) suet or vegetable fat
5 oz (140g) fresh wholemeal breadcrumbs
1½ oz (45g) hazelnuts, chopped (no need to skin)
1 small carrot, grated
2 free range eggs
1 tablespoon molasses
strained juice and grated rind of 1 lemon
water to mix

American

½ cup wholewheat self-raising flour
½ level teaspoon ground cinnamon
½ level teaspoon ground nutmeg
¼ level teaspoon ground fennel
¼ level teaspoon sea salt
1 cup dates or figs, finely chopped
1 cup dried pears, finely chopped (remove any hard core)
½ cup crystallized lemon peel and/or pineapple, finely chopped (see page 169)
½ cup raw cane sugar
½ cup suet or vegetable fat
2½ cups fresh wholewheat breadcrumbs
4½ tablespoons hazelnuts, chopped (no need to skin)
1 small carrot, grated
2 free range eggs
1 tablespoon molasses
strained juice and grated rind of 1 lemon
water to mix

1. Sieve flour, spices and salt together and add to fruit, peel, sugar, suet, breadcrumbs, hazelnuts and grated carrot.

2. Beat the eggs and warm the molasses. Add these with the rind and juice of the lemon to the rest of the ingredients. Mix to a dropping consistency with water.

3. Put into two 1½ pint (850ml) oiled pudding basins and cover with a double sheet of oiled greaseproof paper and either a pudding cloth or a layer of foil.

4. Place in a steamer or pan of boiling water to cover ⅔ of the basin.

5. Steam for 5 hours topping up water as necessary. Cool and put clean covers on as before. To serve, reheat for 2 hours.

Note: Dried fruit and peel can be obtained from most health food stores, and vegetable suet can be obtained from Foodwatch. (See list of suppliers on page 256.)

MINCEMEAT

Makes approximately 3 lb (1kg 350g)

Grain Free	Gluten Free	Milk Free	Egg Free

Imperial (Metric)	*American*
14 oz (395g) dates	3 cups dates
¾ lb (340g) dried pears (remove any hard core)	2¼ cups dried pears (remove any hard core)
6 oz (170g) dried bananas	1 cup dried bananas
4 oz (115g) hazelnuts	¾ cup hazelnuts
1 grapefruit	1 grapefruit
1 level teaspoon cinnamon	1 level teaspoon cinnamon
1 level teaspoon nutmeg, grated or ground	1 level teaspoon nutmeg, grated or ground
a little pure natural grapefruit juice	a little pure natural grapefruit juice

1. Cut all fruit into ¼ inch (5mm) strips.

2. Use coarsest blade of a mincer and mince nuts, fruit and grapefruit. Add spices.

3. Mix well and adjust flavour as required.

4. Add enough grapefruit juice to moisten mixture slightly. Put into jars and label. Keep in a cool place or 'fridge.

7.

SPREADS AND SANDWICH FILLINGS

PEANUT BUTTER

Grain Free	Gluten Free	Milk Free	Egg Free

Imperial (Metric)

½ lb (225g) peanuts, shelled
2 tablespoons sunflower oil
pinch of freshly ground sea salt

American

1½ cups peanuts, shelled
2 tablespoons sunflower oil
pinch of freshly ground sea salt

1. Put the peanuts in a single layer on a baking sheet.

2. Bake in the oven at 300°F/150°C (Gas Mark 2) for 20 minutes until browned.

3. Put immediately on to a cold plate and rub off the skins. You can do this with your fingers, or by putting them into a polythene bag and rubbing them together.

4. Put the skinned nuts into a blender and blend until finely ground but quite dry.

5. Add the oil and blend again until smooth. Taste and add salt if necessary.

VEGETARIAN PÂTÉ

Grain Free   Gluten Free   Milk Free

Another idea for packed lunches or to spread on hot toast for tea.

Imperial (Metric)

1 small onion, chopped
2 celery sticks, finely chopped
1 turnip or carrot, finely chopped
1 clove of garlic, crushed
1 tablespoon safflower or sunflower oil
4 oz (115g) cashew nuts, ground
2 oz (55g) toasted sesame seeds, ground
1 teaspoon dried rosemary
½ teaspoon dried thyme
1 tablespoon natural wheat-free soya sauce (tamari)
sea salt and freshly ground pepper
1 free range egg

American

1 small onion, chopped
2 celery stalks, finely chopped
1 turnip or carrot, finely chopped
1 clove of garlic, crushed
1 tablespoon safflower or sunflower oil
¾ cup cashew nuts, ground
½ cup toasted sesame seeds, ground
1 teaspoon dried rosemary
½ teaspoon dried thyme
1 tablespoon natural wheat-free soy sauce (tamari)
sea salt and freshly ground pepper
1 free range egg

1. Sauté the onion, celery, turnip or carrot and crushed garlic in the oil for a few minutes until soft. Mix with the remaining ingredients and liquidize until smooth.

2. Grease a small ovenproof dish and spoon in the mixture, smoothing the top with a knife.

3. Bake in the oven at 350°F/180°C (Gas Mark 4) for 40 minutes until firm to touch. Leave to cool in the dish, then turn out on to a plate if required.

HUMMUS

Grain Free	Gluten Free	Milk Free	Egg Free

Imperial (Metric)	American
4 oz (115g) chick peas	½ cup garbanzo beans
1 clove garlic	1 clove garlic
1 tablespoon safflower or sunflower oil	1 tablespoon safflower or sunflower oil
1 tablespoon sesame paste (tahini)	1 tablespoon sesame paste (tahini)
juice of a large lemon	juice of a large lemon
sea salt	sea salt
1 tablespoon chopped parsley	1 tablespoon chopped parsley

1. Soak the chick peas (garbanzos) overnight. Drain, cover with fresh water, and bring to the boil. Simmer until tender for 1-2 hours depending on the batch, or cook in a pressure cooker for 30 minutes.

2. Put the garlic, oil, sesame paste and lemon juice into the liquidizer. Liquidize together then gradually add the chick peas, adding some of the cooking liquid to enable the liquidizer to work. Add sea salt and more lemon juice to taste if necessary. Sprinkle the chopped parsley on the top.

Notes:

1. If you haven't any sesame paste, grind 1 tablespoon of sesame seeds in a grinder, then mix with safflower or sunflower oil until it is the required thickness.

2. Serve hummus as a dip, using strips of raw carrot or celery. Put it into pitta bread, with lettuce, watercress or cress, or for a good sandwich filling.

3. This freezes well, so you can make a big batch and freeze it. You can also use haricot or butter beans for this recipe.

HOMEMADE TOFU

Grain Free	Gluten Free	Milk Free	Egg Free

This is a very versatile food, which can be used in many ways. You can slice it, dip it into flour and fry it, then sprinkle with natural soya (soy) sauce. You can use it in cheesecakes, or in pancakes and cakes, or make it into dips, or mayonnaise.

Imperial (Metric)

17.6 fl oz (500ml) carton soya milk
juice of 2 medium sized lemons

American

2¼ cups soy milk
juice of 2 medium sized lemons

1. Heat the soya (soy) milk and remove it when it rises in the pan.

2. Stir in the lemon juice, mixing vigorously, and continue to stir for about ½ minute. The milk should now have separated into curds and whey.

3. Pour into a muslin bag and hang to drip for several hours. If you are storing the tofu, it should be kept in water in the 'fridge, and it will keep for about a week like this.

Note: Ready-made tofu can be purchased in many health food shops. Choose firm tofu for slicing etc. and silken tofu for creaming.

VEGETABLE CREAM CHEESE

Grain Free	Gluten Free	Milk Free	Egg Free

Prepare as above, adding 2 teaspoons of safflower or sunflower oil to the tofu, then sea salt to taste and you have a tasty cream cheese. For added flavour you can add chopped chives, parsley, celery seed or other herbs. Serve on dry biscuits or in salads.

PEAR BLENDER

| Grain Free | Gluten Free | Milk Free | Egg Free |

This makes a lovely spread and it is much better than jam as it contains less sugar.

Imperial (Metric)

1 lb (455g) pears
4 oz (115g) dates
juice of 1 lime
2 tablespoons honey

American

1 pound pears
1 cup dates
juice of 1 lime
2 tablespoons honey

1. Wash the pears very thoroughly, remove cores but do not peel.

2. Chop the dates and pears roughly.

3. Place in a blender with the lime juice and honey.

4. Blend until the mixture is a thick purée.

Note: Serve as a sweet with equal parts of plain yogurt, or spread on bread or biscuits.

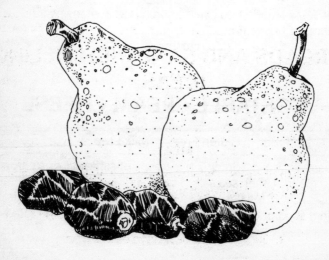

HAZELNUT HONEY SPREAD

Grain Free	Gluten Free	Milk Free	Egg Free

This is a very quick spread to make, providing you have a grinder. Ideal if you've run out of ideas for tea. It's packed with protein.

Imperial (Metric)

4 oz (115g) hazelnuts
1½-2 tablespoons clear honey

American

¾ cup hazelnuts
1½-2 tablespoons clear honey

1. Toast the hazelnuts under the grill for a minute or two, turning frequently as they burn easily.

2. Grind until fine, then mix well with the honey. If the mixture is too thick, thin with a little water.

3. Store in a screw top jar in the refrigerator.

Note: For another flavour you can add a tablespoon of carob powder.

SPREADS AND SANDWICH FILLING IDEAS

MEAT

1. Chicken or turkey, finely chopped and mixed with a little softened milk free margarine or butter to bind.

2. Chicken, peanut butter and Chinese leaves.

3. Turkey, sliced pear and yeast extract.

FISH

1. Well mashed tinned fish (eg. sardines, tuna, salmon) with a squeeze of lemon juice.

2. Tuna or sardines, lettuce and chopped parsley.

3. Crab, watercress and sliced or chopped mushrooms.

4. White fish, fennel and lettuce.

LEFT OVERS

1. Any left over meat or bean casserole (well flavoured) will set thick in the fridge overnight and can be mashed or liquidized.

2. Broken up burgers or rissoles and chives and/or mustard and cress.

NUTS AND SEEDS

1. To make a nut spread put chosen nuts in liquidizer, grind and add water (bottled or filtered if necessary) to make a spreading consistency. Cashews are good to start with, then get braver and try brazils or hazelnuts.

2. Cashew nut spread and celery.

3. Hazelnut spread and sliced pears.

4. Tahini (sesame spread), lettuce and bean sprouts.

5. Sunflower seed spread, mashed banana and coconut.

6. Sunflower seed spread and chopped figs.

FRUITS AND VEGETABLES

1. Mashed banana, chopped nuts and dates.

2. Mashed banana, mixed with a little carob powder.

3. Yeast extract and cooked mashed vegetables.

4. Yeast extract and cooked mashed pulses, mixed with a pinch of curry powder and watercress.

EGG

1. Well mashed hard boiled egg, with a little softened milk free margarine to bind it. You could also use permitted oil and lemon juice or permitted mayonnaise.

2. Hard boiled egg, chopped and mixed with mayonnaise and Chinese leaves.

3. Scrambled egg made with water and cooked sweetcorn and runner beans.

CHEESE

Ricotta is soft and white like curd or cottage cheese. It is sometimes made with cow's or goat's milk but the real 'stuff' is made with sheep's milk. It can be flavoured with chopped parsley, chives etc. or sprouted mung beans, permitted chopped nuts, dates or figs, ground sesame and/or sunflower seeds.
Feta cheese is usually made with sheep's milk, but it can also be made with goat's or cow's milk. A fairly hard white cheese, which can be grated.
Etorki is firm and pale yellow, rather like Edam or Gouda. It slices or grates nicely, and is made with sheep's milk.
Goat's milk cheese is like ricotta, or is available as a hard cheese, although this is more difficult to obtain.
Check all cheeses for additives and to see whether they suit your particular allergies. Cheese may be tolerated when made with vegetable rennet and not calf rennet.

1. Use quark, curd or cottage cheese in place of butter.

2. Cottage cheese, melon or grapefruit with a sprinkling of ginger.

3. Cottage cheese with pineapple and bean sprouts.

4. Cream cheese and sliced pears.

5. Cream cheese with pineapple and walnuts (English walnuts).

6. Cream or cottage cheese with chopped dates and nuts.

7. Grated cheese, chutney (see recipe on page 192), and bean sprouts or young tender spinach.

8. Grated cheese, sliced or chopped mushrooms and spring onions (scallions).

9. Scrambled egg and cottage cheese mixed together with fresh fennel.

Sandwiches can be toasted in cold weather.

GRAIN- OR GLUTEN-FREE PACKED LUNCHES

Select your own choice of salad ingredients (most sandwich fillings can be used) and pack in tubs. (Margarine tubs are useful and free.)

Sweets/puddings can also be packed in tubs. For instance:

1. Fruit — any permitted fresh, stewed or canned, cut up and put in tubs with their own juices or other permitted pure juices. Experiment with flavours to add variety.
Top with yogurt, custard, even cold ground rice milk pudding is nice and filling too (carry toppings in separate tub to stop curdling).

2. Millet pudding or ground rice pudding. These can be carried hot in food flasks.

3. Jellies — made in tubs if possible.

4. Flans, crumbles or breads made with permitted grains.

5. Pieces of melon or pineapple.

6. Dates, figs, permitted fruit and/or nut bars. Biscuits and crisps (potato chips) if allowed.

7. Take a selection of nuts and/or seeds — sunflower, sesame and dill seeds are delicious.

8. Permitted cake or biscuits.

KATH'S GRAPEFRUIT MARMALADE

Makes approximately 3 lb (1kg 350g)

Grain Free	Gluten Free	Milk Free	Egg Free

Imperial (Metric)

2 large grapefruit
1 large lemon
1½ pints (850ml) water
1½ lb (680g) raw cane sugar

American

2 large grapefruit
1 large lemon
3¾ cups water
4 cups raw cane sugar

1. Scrub the fruit, then put into a saucepan with the water. Boil gently with the lid on, for 30 minutes until the fruit is soft.

2. Remove the fruit from the pan, saving the water. Cut in half and scrape out the fruit pulp, pips and some pith, and put in a separate container.

3. Cut the peel to small matchstick-sized strips, or mince it, then put it back into the saucepan with the cooking water.

4. Take the pips and pieces of segment skin and boil in another saucepan with a little water for 15 minutes to release the pectin.

5. Drain and add the water to the shredded peel, with the rest of the fruit pulp.

6. Add the sugar and boil until setting time is reached, usually about 15-30 minutes.

7. Pot and cover with waxed paper. Seal when cold.

FIG AND LEMON PRESERVE

Makes 4 lb (1.8kg)

Grain Free   Gluten Free   Milk Free   Egg Free

Imperial (Metric)

2 lbs (900g) dried figs
2 pints (1,140ml) cold water
rind and juice of 4 lemons
1½ lbs (680g) raw cane sugar

American

6½ cups dried figs
5 cups cold water
rind and juice of 4 lemons
4 cups raw cane sugar

1. Wash the figs, remove stalks, and cut into pieces. Put into a bowl and cover with the water, then leave to soak overnight.

2. Put into a large saucepan or preserving pan, add the strained lemon juice and grated rind, and the sugar.

3. Bring slowly to the boil, stirring to dissolve the sugar, then boil well for 15-20 minutes until setting time is reached.

4. Pour into warm jars while still hot, and cover with waxed paper. Seal when cold.

LEMON CURD

Grain Free   Gluten Free

Imperial (Metric)

2 lemons, scrubbed
½ lb (225g) raw cane sugar
4 oz (115g) unsalted butter
2 free range eggs

American

2 lemons, scrubbed
1⅓ cups raw cane sugar
½ cup unsalted butter
2 free range eggs

1. Put the juice and grated rind of the lemons, the sugar and butter into a basin. Stand in a saucepan of boiling water, or use a double saucepan, and gently heat.

2. While this is heating, beat the eggs and stir into the melted

ingredients, then cook gently until mixture thickens. Do not allow the curd to boil.

3. Pot and cover with waxed paper. Seal when cold.

MELON AND GINGER JAM

Makes approximately 2½-3 lb (1.3-1.8 kilos)

Grain Free   **Gluten Free**   **Milk Free**   **Egg Free**

Buy the melons when they are at their cheapest, otherwise this could be rather an expensive jam. Choose fruit that is not too ripe.

Imperial (Metric)	*American*
1 *large melon (approximately 3 lb to make 1½ lb (680g) of fruit when cut away from the skin)*	1 *large melon (approximately 3 pounds to make 1½ pounds of fruit when cut away from the skin)*
¾ *lb (340g) raw cane sugar*	2 *cups raw cane sugar*
2 *tablespoons lemon juice, plus the peel and white pith of the lemon*	2 *tablespoons lemon juice, plus the peel and white pith of the lemon*
1 *oz (30g) bruised root ginger or*	1 *ounce bruised root ginger or*
1 *teaspoon powdered ginger*	1 *teaspoon powdered ginger*

1. Quarter the melon. Scrape out the pips, cut the fruit away from the skin, and cube.

2. Put into a bowl and cover with the sugar, then leave overnight for the juice to be extracted.

3. Place the pith and peel of the lemon, and the bruised root ginger in a muslin bag.

4. Put the fruit and sugar mixture in a preserving pan with the muslin bag, and fast boil until setting time is reached. This may be after only 5 minutes. When testing for setting always remove the pan from the heat, otherwise you may boil past setting time.

5. Pot and cover with waxed papers, and seal when cold.

Note: Using the same method you can make marrow and ginger jam.

RHUBARB AND LEMON JAM

Makes 2 lb (900g)

| Grain Free | Gluten Free | Milk Free | Egg Free |

Imperial (Metric)

1 lb (455g) rhubarb
juice and peel of 2 lemons (scrub
  skins well)
1 lb (455g) raw cane sugar

American

1 pound rhubarb
juice and peel of 2 lemons (scrub
  skins well)
2⅔ cups raw cane sugar

1. Clean the rhubarb and cut it up into small pieces. Add strained lemon juice. Simmer gently in a saucepan or preserving pan.

2. When the fruit is soft add the sugar and finely chopped lemon peel.

3. Boil fast until setting time is reached. To check this, remove the jam from the heat and drop a little on to a cold plate. Leave until cold then push with finger tip. If setting time has been reached, the jam will crinkle. If this does not happen, boil the jam fast for a few more minutes. Remove scum.

4. Allow to cool slightly then put into clean jars, and put on waxed papers. When cold cover with transparent covers.

PICCALILLI

Milk Free   Egg Free

This is an easy pickle to make, once you've done all the preparation.

Imperial (Metric)

1 lb (455g) cauliflower florets and stalk cut into ½ inch (1cm) slices

1 lb (455g) marrow cut into ½ inch (1cm) chunks

½ lb (225g) onions, chopped

½ lb (225g) celery, cut into small pieces

½ lb (225g) cabbage, red or white, sliced

½ lb (225g) beans, sliced (French, runner or broad)

6 oz (170g) raw cane sugar

2 oz (55g) wholemeal plain flour

1 oz (30g) dry mustard

1 tablespoon turmeric

1 teaspoon ground ginger

2 pints (1.14 litres) distilled white vinegar

American

1 pound cauliflower florets and stalk cut into ½ inch (1cm) slices

1 pound summer squash cut into ½ inch (1cm) chunks

1⅓ cups onions, chopped

1⅓ cups celery, cut into small pieces

2 cups cabbage, red or white, sliced

½ pound beans, sliced (snap, green beans, Windsor or fava beans)

1 cup raw cane sugar

½ cup wholewheat plain flour

2½ tablespoons dry mustard

1 tablespoon turmeric

1 teaspoon ground ginger

5 cups distilled white vinegar

1. Prepare the vegetables.

2. Blend the dry ingredients with a little of the vinegar to make a thin cream, then stir in the rest of the vinegar. Cook, stirring well, until the vinegar mixture thickens. Add the vegetables and simmer, stirring occasionally, for 15 minutes.

3. Put into prepared jars and cover when cold.

FRUITY CHUTNEY

| Grain Free | Gluten Free | Milk Free | Egg Free |

Imperial (Metric)

½ lb (225g) dates
½ lb (225g) pears
½ lb (225g) onions
2 celery sticks
6 oz (170g) raw cane sugar
sea salt and freshly ground pepper
½ pint (285ml) white vinegar

American

1½ cups dates
1½ cups pears
1⅓ cups onions
2 celery stalks
1 cup raw cane sugar
sea salt and freshly ground pepper
1⅓ cups white vinegar

1. Mince together dates, pears, onions and celery. Stir in sugar and add ½ teaspoon salt, and a good taste of pepper.

2. Pour over the vinegar and leave for 24 hours in a covered bowl, stirring occasionally.

3. Pot and store in a dry cupboard. This keeps a long time and is delicious.

Note: A tablespoon of chutney mixed with 2 tablespoons of plain natural yogurt makes a tasty salad dressing.

PEAR AND CHIVE RELISH

Grain Free   Gluten Free   Milk Free   Egg Free

Imperial (Metric)

1 lb (455g) pears
½ lb (225g) onions
½ pint (285ml) distilled white
 vinegar
6 oz (170g) raw cane sugar
2 tablespoons chopped fresh chives
¼ teaspoon sea salt

American

1 pound pears
1⅓ cups onions
1⅓ cups distilled white vinegar
1 cup raw cane sugar
2 tablespoons chopped fresh chives
¼ teaspoon sea salt

1. Wash, core but do not peel the pears, and cut into small dice. Chop the onions into small pieces.

2. Put the pears and onion into a saucepan with the vinegar and cook gently until just soft, about 15 minutes.

3. Stir in the sugar, chives and salt and cook fairly fast for another 15 minutes until thickened.

4. Pot and cover. Serve with cheese and biscuits, or burgers, etc.

SPICED VINEGAR

| Grain Free | Gluten Free | Milk Free | Egg Free |

Use whole spices for maximum flavour and clarity.

Imperial (Metric)	American
¼ oz (7g) cardamom	½ teaspoon cardamom
¼ oz (7g) cinnamon	½ teaspoon cinnamon
¼ oz (7g) coriander	½ teaspoon coriander
¼ oz (7g) whole nutmeg	½ teaspoon whole nutmeg
¼ oz (7g) ginger (root)	½ teaspoon ginger (root)
¼ oz (7g) black peppercorns	½ teaspoon black peppercorns
6 bay leaves	6 bay leaves
2 pints (1.14 litres) white vinegar	5 cups white vinegar

1. Crush spices with pestle and mortar or rolling pin.

2. Place crushed spices in a muslin bag with vinegar and bring to boiling point but do not boil. Keep a lid on the pan.

3. Remove from the heat and leave for 2½ hours. It is now fully spiced and ready for use.

4. Bottle and keep in a cool place.

8.

SPECIAL OCCASIONS

PARTY IDEAS

1. Pieces of celery filled with Quark or peanut butter.

2. Cheese and pineapple on cocktail sticks.

3. Half a walnut, and cube of cheese on a cocktail stick.

4. Mini pizzas (see pizza recipe on page 48).

5. Pizza potatoes — Make a ratatouille topping with one onion, one garlic clove and courgettes (zucchini). Spread on a baked potato, add a slice of cheese, and chopped mushrooms. Grill until the cheese melts.

6. Homemade vegetable pasties — Make shortcrust or flaky pastry and fill with cooked mixed vegetables such as onions, carrots, potatoes, celery, turnips, mushrooms and courgettes (zucchini), and a clove of garlic if liked. Mix with some cooked pulses or cooked rice and vegetable stock and bake.

7. Savoury Rolls (see page 198).

8. Savoury Sesame Sticks (see page 199).

CRUDITÉS

Children seem to enjoy dipping and the slices of vegetables make a healthy colourful addition to the party table. Try serving these vegetables with one of the dips that follow:

Carrots: Cut into thick matchstick shapes, or slice horizontally and cut out shapes with a small biscuit cutter.

Mushrooms: Peel the mushrooms, trim the stalks, then cut into thick slices.

Celery: Cut into thin matchsticks.

Radishes: Red or white.

Spring Onions (Scallions): Trim and cut into appropriate lengths.

Turnips: Cut into sticks.

Chinese leaves: Use the thicker white parts nearer to the base.

Pieces of pineapple.

Cauliflower florets.

SESAME DIP

Grain Free	Gluten Free	Milk Free	Egg Free

Sesame seeds are an excellent source of calcium.

Imperial (Metric)

2 tablespoons tahini (sesame paste)
1 clove garlic, crushed
2 tablespoons finely chopped parsley
3 tablespoons lemon juice
1 teaspoon wheat free tamari (soya sauce)

American

2 tablespoons tahini (sesame paste)
1 clove garlic, crushed
2 tablespoons finely chopped parsley
3 tablespoons lemon juice
1 teaspoon wheat free tamari (soy sauce)

1. Mix all the ingredients well together. Add a little extra oil if the dip is too thick.

QUARK DIP

Grain Free	Gluten Free	Egg Free

Imperial (Metric)

8 oz (225g) Quark cheese
2 tablespoons chopped parsley or
   chives
freshly ground pepper

American

1 cup Quark cheese
2 tablespoons chopped parsley or
   chives
freshly ground pepper

1. Mix all the ingredients together.

AVOCADO DIP

Grain Free	Gluten Free	Milk Free	Egg Free

You could also use this as a salad dressing, or it is very good on
   baked potatoes. It is high in protein, vitamins and minerals.

Imperial (Metric)

1 ripe avocado
1 clove of garlic
1 teaspoon wheat free tamari (soya
   sauce) or more to taste
5 oz (140g) silken tofu
2 tablespoons lime juice
½ teaspoon sea salt
1 tablespoon safflower or sunflower
   oil

American

1 ripe avocado
1 clove of garlic
1 teaspoon wheat free tamari (soy
   sauce) or more to taste
⅔ cup silken tofu
2 tablespoons lime juice
½ teaspoon sea salt
1 tablespoon safflower or sunflower
   oil

1. Whip or liquidize the ingredients together.

SAVOURY ROLLS

Imperial (Metric)

4 oz (115g) dried butter beans
2 oz (55g) carrot, grated
2 sticks of celery, finely chopped
1 teaspoon dried mixed herbs
sea salt and freshly ground pepper
2 tablespoons toasted sesame seeds
1 teaspoon yeast extract
1 egg yolk, free range
egg white for brushing pastry

American

⅔ cup dried lima beans
½ cup carrot, grated
2 stalks of celery, finely chopped
1 teaspoon dried mixed herbs
sea salt and freshly ground pepper
2 tablespoons toasted sesame seeds
1 teaspoon yeast extract
1 egg yolk, free range
egg white for brushing pastry

Pastry:

Imperial (Metric)

10 oz (285g) wholemeal flour
5 oz (140g) margarine
2 teaspoons lemon juice
water to mix

American

2½ cups wholewheat flour
½ cup + 2½ tablespoons margarine
2 teaspoons lemon juice
water to mix

1. Wash the beans and soak overnight.

2. Cook the beans for 1-1½ hours until soft.

3. Mince or mash together with the grated carrot, chopped celery, mixed herbs, sea salt and pepper and sesame seeds.

4. Mix the yeast extract with the egg yolk, then add to the mixture.

5. Make the pastry by rubbing the fat in to the flour, and mix in the lemon juice with enough water to form a stiff dough.

6. Roll out into a long strip, and roll the filling into a long strip the same length as the pastry. Place the filling along the middle of the pastry, brush the edges with water, fold over and seal.

7. Brush the top with egg white and cut into 12 medium pieces or 16 smaller pieces. Make three small slits in each roll and bake in the oven at 400°F/200°C (Gas Mark 6) for 20 minutes.

SAVOURY SESAME STICKS

Makes about 40

Egg Free

Imperial (Metric)	American
½ lb (225g) wholemeal flour	2 cups wholewheat flour
4 oz (115g) margarine	½ cup margarine
2 tablespoons ground sesame seeds	2 tablespoons ground sesame seeds
freshly ground pepper	freshly ground pepper
water to mix	water to mix
2 teaspoons yeast extract	2 teaspoons yeast extract
2 teaspoons hot water	2 teaspoons hot water
2 tablespoons sesame seeds	2 tablespoons sesame seeds

1. Rub the fat into the flour, ground sesame seeds and pepper.

2. Mix with a little water to make a dough.

3. Take small pieces, about the size of a large teaspoon, and roll between the palms into thin sticks about 6 inches (15cm) long.

4. Put on to a greased baking tray.

5. Mix the yeast extract with the water, and brush liberally on to the sticks. Sprinkle on the sesame seeds.

6. Bake in the oven at 425°P/220°C (Gas Mark 7) for 10-15 minutes until crisp.

FRUITY FATHER CHRISTMAS

This is a recipe that the children will really enjoy helping to make. Use any allowed dried fruit such as dried pears, figs or dates. You could also add walnuts (English walnuts) or chopped stem or crystallized ginger.

For the dough:
Follow the recipe and method for Hot Cross Buns (see page 168), save a date to make the eyes, nose and mouth, and divide the mixture into 3 pieces.

For the Icing:

Imperial (Metric)	**American**
4 oz (115g) pack Coconut Cream	1 cup Coconut Cream
1 tablespoon raw cane sugar or honey	1 tablespoon raw cane sugar or honey
beetroot juice (see page 19)	beetroot juice (see page 19)

1. Make the first ball of dough into an oval for the body 6×4 inches (15×10cm) and put on to a greased baking sheet.

2. Make the second ball of dough into a sack and head with a hat on.

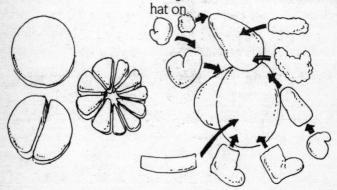

3. Make the third ball of dough into ten pieces, four larger pieces to make the arms and boots, and six smaller pieces to make two hands, one pompom, one beard, one belt and one hat band.

4. Add the head, sack, arms and boots to the body, then the hands, pompom, beard, belt and hatband.

5. Use pieces of date to make the eyes, nose and mouth.

6. Leave to rise in a warm place covered with a cloth until doubled in size (about 35 minutes).

7. Bake in the oven at 425°F/220°C (Gas Mark 7) for 20-25 minutes.

8. Remove very carefully from the baking tray (it may be easier to use two spatulas) and cool on a wire rack.

9. Grate the coconut cream and heat with the sugar or honey in enough water to make a thick smooth cream. Reserve enough white cream to cover the pompom, hat band, beard, belt and boots. Mix the beetroot juice with the remaining cream, and spread over the body, arms and hat. Spread the remaining white cream over the beard, pompom, hat band, belt and boots.

PINEAPPLE AND GINGER MACAROON GATEAU

Gluten Free

The strained Greek yogurt makes a lovely filling, and you can get it made from cow's or sheep's milk.

Imperial (Metric)	*American*
4 egg whites, free range	4 egg whites, free range
3 oz (85g) ground raw cane sugar	½ cup ground raw cane sugar
4 oz (115g) finely ground hazelnuts	¾ cup finely ground hazelnuts
1 teaspoon brown rice flour	1 tablespoon brown rice flour
rice paper	rice paper

For the filling:

Imperial (Metric)	*American*
½ lb (225g) tin pineapple pieces in their own juice, or fresh pineapple pieces	½ pound can pineapple pieces in their own juice, or fresh pineapple pieces
½ lb (225g) strained Greek yogurt (or any thick set yogurt)	1 cup strained Greek yogurt (or any thick set yogurt)
2 oz (55g) chopped crystallized or stem ginger	2 tablespoons chopped crystallized or stem ginger

1. Turn the oven to 275°F/140°C (Gas Mark 1). Line one or two large well oiled baking tins with rice paper.

2. Whisk the egg whites until they are stiff and will form soft peaks. Add two tablespoons of sugar and continue to whisk for about a minute. Gently fold in the rest of the sugar, ground hazelnuts and rice flour.

3. Spread the mixture into three thin circles 6-7 inches (15-18cm) in diameter on the rice paper.

4. Bake in the pre-set oven for 1-1¼ hours until they are crisp, then leave in the switched off oven for an hour to dry thoroughly. Cool and store in an airtight tin.

5. It is best to fill the circles about 2-3 hours before serving, so that they will be soft enough to cut.

6. Fill the circles as you would a gateau. Divide the yogurt into three, then put a layer between each circle adding the pineapple and ginger pieces. Spread the top with yogurt and decorate with the remaining pineapple and ginger pieces.

PUMPKIN PIE

Cut out the flesh from the pumpkin, and make a pumpkin pie for Halloween, then use the shell to make a Jack O'Lantern face. To cook the pumpkin it is best to cut the flesh into small pieces, then simmer in very little water or steam it until it is tender. Drain off the liquid, then mash to a purée.

Imperial (Metric)

½ lb (225g) shortcrust pastry (see page 148)
¾ lb (340g) pumpkin purée
2 oz (55g) raw cane sugar
1 teaspoon ground cinnamon
½ teaspoon ground nutmeg
¼ pint (140ml) milk (cow's, goat's or soya)
3 free range eggs, separated
3 oz (85g) chopped dried fruit (dates, figs or pears)

American

½ pound shortcrust pastry (see page 148)
1½ cups pumpkin purée
⅓ cup raw cane sugar
1 teaspoon ground cinnamon
½ teaspoon ground nutmeg
⅔ cup milk (cow's, goat's or soy)
3 free range eggs, separated
½ cup chopped dried fruit (dates, figs or pears)

1. Make the pastry and line a 10 inch (25cm) pie dish.

2. Mix the pumpkin purée with the sugar, spices, milk and egg yolks and purée in a liquidizer until smooth.

3. Mix in the dried fruit.

4. Whisk the egg whites until stiff then fold into the pumpkin mixture. Pour into the unbaked pastry shell and bake at 375°F/190°C (Gas Mark 5) for 45-60 minutes until firm.

PROFITEROLES WITH CAROB SAUCE

Makes about 20

Gluten Free

This recipe uses rice flour and makes deliciously light crisp profiteroles. You can of course use wholemeal (wholewheat) flour if preferred.

Imperial (Metric)	American
2 oz (55g) unsalted butter	¼ cup unsalted butter
¼ pint (140ml) water	⅔ cup water
2 oz (55g) brown rice flour	3 tablespoons brown rice flour
pinch sea salt	pinch sea salt
2 free range eggs	2 free range eggs
¼ pint (140ml) double cream or	⅔ cup heavy cream or
½ lb (225g) strained Greek yogurt	1 cup strained Greek yogurt

For the sauce:

Imperial (Metric)	American
1 tablespoon carob powder, sieved	1 tablespoon carob powder, sieved
1 tablespoon ground raw cane sugar	1 tablespoon ground raw cane sugar
1 teaspoon safflower or sunflower oil	1 teaspoon safflower or sunflower oil
1 tablespoon water	1 tablespoon water

1. Melt the butter in the water and bring to the boil. Remove from the heat immediately and stir in the flour and salt. Beat with a wooden spoon until a soft ball is formed and the mixture leaves the sides of the pan.

2. Beat in the eggs one at a time, making sure each egg is absorbed before adding the next. The mixture should be smooth and glossy.

3. Put the mixture in teaspoon-sized balls on to a greased baking tray. Bake in the oven at 350°F/180°C (Gas Mark 4) for 30 minutes. They should be crisp and lightly browned on top.

4. Remove from the oven and slit each one to let the steam escape.

5. Cool on a wire rack.

6. Blend the sauce ingredients together over a gentle heat. Whip the cream if used, and fill the profiteroles with either the cream or yogurt. Spread the sauce on the tops. Can be frozen after adding the cream and sauce.

TROPICAL PINEAPPLE FRUIT SALAD

Grain Free	Gluten Free	Milk Free	Egg Free

Imperial (Metric)

1 *fresh pineapple*
*fruits of choice eg. mangoes, papayas
    (paw paw), persimmons, bananas,
    melon or watermelon, guavas,
    dates, pomegranates, grated
    coconut*

American

1 *fresh pineapple*
*fruits of choice eg. mangoes, papayas
    (paw paw), Sharon fruit, bananas,
    melon or watermelon, guavas,
    dates, pomegranates, grated
    coconut*

1. Slice the top off the pineapple, hollow out the flesh and place in a mixing bowl.

2. Take out the hard middle core, and any discoloured parts.

3. Cut the pineapple flesh and the fruits of your choice into bite sized pieces and put back into the pineapple shell.

4. Replace the top and serve chilled.

Note: If you prefer you could do the same thing using a melon.

CARROT CAKE

This makes a nourishing, moist, orange-coloured cake.

Imperial (Metric)	American
½ lb (225g) wholemeal flour	2 cups wholewheat flour
3 teaspoons baking powder	3 teaspoons baking powder
3 oz (85g) raw cane sugar	½ cup raw cane sugar
4 oz (115g) grated carrot	1 cup grated carrot
2 ripe bananas, mashed	2 ripe bananas, mashed
2 oz (55g) walnuts, chopped	½ cup English walnuts, chopped
1 teaspoon ground cinnamon	1 teaspoon ground cinnamon
a pinch of ground nutmeg	a pinch of ground nutmeg
2 free range eggs	2 free range eggs
¼ pint (140ml) safflower or sunflower oil	⅔ cup safflower or sunflower oil

Topping:

Imperial (Metric)	American
½ lb (225g) Quark or strained Greek yogurt	1 cup Quark or strained Greek yogurt
2 tablespoons clear honey	2 tablespoons clear honey
1 teaspoon natural vanilla essence	1 teaspoon natural vanilla essence
walnuts to decorate	English walnuts to decorate

1. Put the flour, baking powder and sugar into a mixing bowl. Stir in the carrots, mashed bananas, walnuts (English walnuts), cinnamon and nutmeg.

2. Mix the eggs and oil together and add to the mixture, beating well until thoroughly blended.

3. Put into an oiled 8 inch (20cm) round cake tin. Bake at 350°F/180°C (Gas Mark 4) for 1¼ hours or until the cake shrinks from the sides of the tin. Cool on a wire rack.

4. Beat the topping ingredients together until smooth.

5. Spread over the top of the cooled cake, decorating with a fork. Add walnut (English walnut) halves.

CRISPY SPICY NUTS

Grain Free   Gluten Free   Milk Free

Imperial (Metric)	*American*
4 oz (115g) mixed nuts, eg. peanuts, cashew nuts, hazelnuts, sunflower seeds or pumpkin seeds	¾ cup mixed nuts, eg. peanuts, cashew nuts, hazelnuts, sunflower seeds or pumpkin seeds
1 egg white, free range	1 egg white, free range
1 tablespoon chickpea flour	1 tablespoon gram flour
½ teaspoon sea salt	½ teaspoon sea salt
¼ teaspoon freshly ground pepper	¼ teaspoon freshly ground pepper
¼-½ teaspoon garlic salt	¼-½ teaspoon garlic salt
½ teaspoon ground cumin	½ teaspoon ground cumin
½ teaspoon ground coriander	½ teaspoon ground coriander
½ teaspoon ground turmeric	½ teaspoon ground turmeric
2 tablespoons safflower or sunflower oil	2 tablespoons safflower or sunflower oil

1. Remove the skins from the nuts where necessary. For peanuts and hazelnuts, put into a flat baking tin and bake at 350°F/180°C (Gas Mark 4) for 15 minutes. Rub with a clean tea towel to remove the skins.

2. Coat the nuts in the egg white.

3. Mix the flour, sea salt and pepper, garlic salt and spices, then sift the mixture over the nuts.

4. Heat the oil and stir fry the nuts at a high heat for 2-3 minutes until they look crisp and golden. Drain on white kitchen paper and store in an airtight container.

GUAVA LIME ICE CREAM

Grain Free   Gluten Free   Milk Free

We have tried not to include tinned (canned) food in this book because of the danger of lead contamination from the lead solder in some tins (cans), but as fresh guavas are very hard to obtain, it is probably easier to use tinned (canned) guavas on this occasion.

Imperial (Metric)

¾ pint (425ml) soya milk
4 egg yolks, free range
2 oz (55g) ground raw cane sugar
½ lb (225g) drained guavas
juice of 1 lime (choose the more
   yellow ones as they are juicier)

American

2 cups soy milk
4 egg yolks, free range
⅓ cup ground raw cane sugar
½ pound drained guavas
juice of 1 lime (choose the more
   yellow ones as they are juicier)

1. Heat the milk to the boil, then allow to cool for 2-3 minutes.

2. Whisk in the egg yolks and sugar. Reheat very gently, stirring all the time, until the custard thickens and coats the back of a spoon. Do not let it boil or it will curdle.

3. Remove the seeds from the guavas and liquidize together with the lime juice, or purée using a sieve.

4. When the custard has cooled add the guava purée to it, mixing well.

5. Pour into a freezer tray.

6. During freezing time remove from the freezer and whisk well, then continue freezing.

ICE LOLLIES (POPSICLES)

Grain Free   Gluten Free   Milk Free   Egg Free

Pineapple — Add a few drops of lemon juice to unsweetened pineapple juice to taste. Freeze in ice lolly (popsicle) containers.

Grapefruit — (Makes 2) Squeeze the juice from a grapefruit, and add 2 teaspoons of honey. You may have to warm the mixture a little to combine the two. Put in ice lolly (popsicle) containers and freeze.

WHEATFLAKE CRACKELETS

Egg Free

Imperial (Metric)

1 oz (30g) unsalted butter or margarine
1 tablespoon raw cane sugar
1 tablespoon molasses or black treacle
2 oz (55g) wholewheat flakes
1 tablespoon hazelnuts, ground or chopped

American

2½ tablespoons unsalted butter or margarine
1 tablespoon raw cane sugar
1 tablespoon molasses
1¼ cups wholewheat flakes
1 tablespoon hazelnuts, ground or chopped

1. Melt the butter, sugar and molasses slowly in a saucepan. Do not allow to boil.

2. Add wheatflakes and nuts. Mix until thoroughly coated.

3. Put into paper cases and leave to set hard.

Note: Use 1 tablespoon of walnuts, coconut, or carob powder instead of hazelnuts.

SUNFLOWER/SESAME BARS

Grain Free   Gluten Free   Egg Free

For a milk free recipe use soya (soy) milk powder.

Imperial (Metric)	American
2 oz (55g) sunflower seeds	½ cup sunflower seeds
2 oz (55g) sesame seeds	½ cup sesame seeds
2 oz (55g) desiccated coconut	⅔ cup desiccated coconut
1 tablespoon dried milk powder (soya if necessary)	1 tablespoon dried milk powder (soy if necessary)
2 tablespoons clear honey	2 tablespoons clear honey

1. Mix all ingredients together thoroughly and put into an oiled ovenproof dish 7 inches (18cm) square.

2. Bake in the oven at 350°F/180°C (Gas Mark 4) for 20 minutes. While still warm score into 12 pieces.

Note: Use any safe nuts or seeds as desired.

FRUITY CAROB CRUNCH

Egg Free

Imperial (Metric)	American
2×2.75 oz (75g) carob bars or 6 oz (170g) carob chips	1 cup carob bars or chips
2 oz (55g) muesli base or rolled oats, from health shops	½ cup muesli base or rolled oats, from health shops
2 oz (55g) chopped cashews	½ cup chopped cashews
2 oz (55g) chopped dates or figs	⅓ cup chopped dates or figs

1. Melt the carob bars in a bowl over hot water.

2. Stir in the other ingredients and mix well.

3. Place spoonsful of the mixture in paper cases and leave to set.

FRUIT BARS

Gluten Free   Milk Free   Egg Free

Imperial (Metric)	American
4 oz (115g) dates	1 cup dates
4 oz (115g) figs	1 cup figs
2 oz (55g) walnuts or brazil nuts	½ cup English walnuts or brazil nuts
2 oz (55g) hazelnuts	½ cup hazelnuts
1 tablespoon lemon juice	1 tablespoon lemon juice
grated rind of 1 lemon	grated rind of 1 lemon

1. Put fruit and nuts through a fine mincer. Mix with lemon juice and rind to make a stiff paste, adding more lemon juice if necessary.

2. Press on to a sheet of rice paper then cover with another piece to make a flat block. Leave overnight to harden, then cut into bar shapes with a sharp knife, dipped in boiling water.

3. Wrap in greaseproof paper and store in a cool place.

Note: You can put in some fresh chopped or preserved ginger to make another flavour.

HONEY HALVA

Grain Free   Gluten Free   Milk Free   Egg Free

This can be made in a minute, but you need a grinder. Sesame seeds are an excellent source of calcium.

Imperial (Metric)	American
4 oz (115g) sesame seeds	1 cup sesame seeds
1 tablespoon clear honey	1 tablespoon clear honey

1. Toast the sesame seeds under the grill for a minute or two, watching carefully as they burn easily.

2. Grind them down in the grinder, then mix in the honey. Make into a slab, then cut into small squares.

POPCORN

Gluten Free   Milk Free   Egg Free

This is ideal for a birthday party. Children love to help make it and listen to the corn popping. Do not lift the lid while popping. It could be very dangerous. Popcorn can be bought cheaply from most health food shops.

1. Put the popping corn into a saucepan with the lid on and heat until the corn pops.

2. Shake the saucepan about to stop corn from burning, as it burns very easily.

3. Either eat plain, sprinkle with melted honey, or add salt, melted butter, herbs, spices or tamari.

Note: You can serve it as a breakfast cereal with honey and milk.

TOFFEE

Grain Free   Gluten Free   Egg Free

Imperial (Metric)	American
½ lb (225g) demerara sugar	1⅓ cups demerara sugar
4 oz (115g) butter (not margarine as it will not work)	½ cup butter (not margarine as it will not work)
2 teaspoons black treacle	2 teaspoons molasses

1. Boil ingredients together for 3-6 minutes until a little of the mixture will set when dropped into cold water.

2. Put into a buttered tin and leave to set.

Note: 2 tablespoons of sesame seeds can be added when setting time is reached to make sesame toffee. Alternatively, add 4 oz (115g, ¾ cup) of brazil nuts or other nuts like walnuts or hazelnuts.

HAZELNUT AND SESAME BRITTLE

Gluten Free   Egg Free

Imperial (Metric)	*American*
4 oz (115g) whole hazelnuts	¾ cup whole hazelnuts
2 tablespoons honey	2 tablespoons honey
1 oz (30g) raw cane sugar	2 tablespoons raw cane sugar
1 oz (30g) butter	2½ tablespoons butter
5 tablespoons water	5 tablespoons water
rice paper	rice paper
4 tablespoons sesame seeds	4 tablespoons sesame seeds

1. Toast the hazelnuts under the grill for a minute or two, watching carefully to prevent them burning. Rub with a clean tea towel to remove the skins.

2. Put the honey, sugar, butter and water into a saucepan. Stir over a low heat, then bring to the boil.

3. Boil until the syrup forms hard brittle threads in cold water, about 8-10 minutes.

4. Meanwhile cut a piece of rice paper approximately 7×8 inches (18×20cm) and put on to a baking tray.

5. Remove the syrup from the heat, then stir in the nuts and seeds, spread on to the rice paper and leave to set.

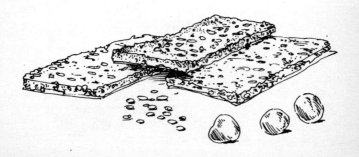

TOFFEE PEARS

Grain Free   Gluten Free   Egg Free

These are good for birthday parties or barbecues, and the children love to help make them. Get some dowel from a hardware store, and cut it into appropriate sized sticks.

Imperial (Metric)

6-8 medium sized firm pears
1 lb (455g) demerara sugar
4 oz (115g) molasses or black treacle
3 oz (85g) butter
2 teaspoons white vinegar
¼ pint (140ml) water
6-8 wooden sticks

American

6-8 medium sized firm pears
2⅔ cups demerara sugar
4 tablespoons molasses
⅓ cup butter
2 teaspoons white vinegar
⅔ cup water
6-8 wooden sticks

1. Wash and dry the pears, and pierce them with the sticks.

2. Put the sugar, treacle or molasses, butter, vinegar and water into a saucepan and heat gently until the sugar has dissolved.

3. Boil quickly for about 5 minutes until the toffee goes hard but not brittle when dropped into cold water, or until the temperature reaches 290°F/143°C.

4. Dip the pears quickly into the toffee, coating them evenly. Stand the pears on greaseproof paper to cool.

HOMEMADE CAROB EASTER EGGS

Grain Free   Gluten Free   Egg Free

Imperial (Metric)

4 oz (115g) carob chips, or bars
2 medium-sized empty egg shells
  with a hole in the top

American

⅔ cup carob chips or bars
2 medium-sized empty egg shells
  with a hole in the top

For the soft centre:

Imperial (Metric)

1 oz (30g) ground hazelnuts or
  walnuts
1 teaspoon honey

American

¼ cup ground hazelnuts or English
  walnuts
1 teaspoon honey

1. Put the carob chips or bars into a basin and stand in a bowl of hot water to melt them.

2. Pour the contents of the eggs into a basin through a hole in the top of the egg. Rinse the egg shells.

3. Mix the nuts with the honey to make two small balls.

4. Stand the egg shells in egg cups and pour the melted carob into the openings until half full. Put in the walnut balls, then the rest of the melted carob. Leave to set.

5. Either serve turned upside down in their shells, pretending they are boiled eggs, or peel and wrap in gold or silver foil, and decorate with flowers.

9.

DRINKS

Tea and coffee are stimulants and can be addictive. The following are useful substitutes. Herbal teas and grain coffees are often an acquired taste so persevere. To make drinks more interesting, make a 'pot of tea for one'.

HERBAL TEAS

These are refreshing and beneficial. They are usually bought packed in tea bags and are made as for ordinary tea. Leave to stand for 10 minutes to infuse. Sweeten if desired with honey. They should be served without milk.

Try some of the following:

Hibiscus — Calming and thirst quenching.

Lime flower — Calming and good for feverish colds.

Chamomile — Calming, soothing for colic stomach pains, etc.

Fennel — Calming, helps appetite.

Lemon Balm (Melissa) and Verbena — Calming, useful for all nervous problems.

COFFEE SUBSTITUTES

Milk Free	Egg Free

BARLEY CUP
Roasted barley, rye and chicory.

GRANOSE SWISS CUP
Roasted rye, oats, millet, barley, figs and chicory.

Grain Free	Gluten Free	Milk Free	Egg Free

PREWETTS CHICORY
100% roasted chicory root.

Grain Free	Gluten Free	Egg Free

SYMINGTONS DANDELION COFFEE
Roasted dandelion root and lactose.

WARNING
Lactose is a form of milk sugar and will affect those with a milk intolerance.

Grain Free	Gluten Free	Milk Free	Egg Free

CAROB POWDER (CHOCOLATE SUBSTITUTE)
Use in place of cocoa for drinks and cooking. Even additive free pure cocoa contains caffeine, a stimulant.

YEAST EXTRACT
Marmite Yeast Extract
Tastex (Granose) Yeast Extract
Natex (Modern Health Products Ltd) Yeast Extract
All contain vitamin B_{12}, important for vegetarians.

MILK

Goat's milk may be accepted in cases of cow's milk allergy — worth a try. It is available fresh, frozen or in powdered form.

Sheep's milk is becoming more widely available and this can sometimes be tolerated better than goat's milk. It freezes well.

SOYA BEAN PLANT MILK

May be used in drinks. Available in cans or cartons with or without raw cane sugar. See also list of suppliers on page 257-263.

FRUIT AND VEGETABLE JUICES

Leisure Drinks. See list of suppliers on pages 257-263.

Prewetts. See list of suppliers on pages 257-263.

Dilute to taste with hot or cold water.

Or make your own juices with an electric or hand juicer.

Homemade drinks.

Filtered water — see page 262.

Mineral water — genuine spring water without additives.

CITRUS FRUIT DRINKS

Grain Free   Gluten Free   Milk Free   Egg Free

---

1. Honey may be used in place of raw cane sugar in any of the following drinks. However, it is better not to add the honey to boiling water as the goodness may be destroyed.

2. All drinks can be stored in clean glass bottles. If plastic containers are needed use white lined containers that have no odour. Coloured containers are not advised.

3. HOT DRINKS
If drinks are needed hot, put required amount into a strong mug. Place mug in a heatproof basin and pour boiling water into basin. Leave until required heat is reached. This method is better than heating the drink in a saucepan directly over heat.

4. 'FRUIT COCKTAIL' DRINKS
Mix any combination of permitted fruit juices together. Add a slice of lemon and ice cubes. Any extra strained juice from permitted stewed fruit can be used, and this makes a good flavoured drink. Stewed, strained fruit juices are also nice on their own.

HAWAIIAN QUENCHER

Grain Free   Gluten Free   Egg Free

This is a really refreshing drink.

Imperial (Metric)	*American*
¼ pint (140ml) natural yogurt	⅔ cup plain yogurt
¼ pint (140ml) pineapple juice	⅔ cup pineapple juice
1 teaspoon clear honey	1 teaspoon clear honey
fresh pineapple cubes	fresh pineapple cubes

1. Whisk the yogurt, pineapple juice and honey together until blended. Serve in tumblers with pineapple cubes.

GRAPEFRUIT DRINK

Grain Free	Gluten Free	Milk Free	Egg Free

Imperial (Metric)

2 tablespoons raw cane sugar
1-1½ pints (570-850ml) boiling
   water
1 grapefruit

American

2 tablespoons raw cane sugar
2½-3¾ cups boiling water
1 grapefruit

1. Stir the sugar into the water and heat until dissolved. Allow to cool then stir in the juice squeezed from the grapefruit.

LEMONADE

Grain Free	Gluten Free	Milk Free	Egg Free

Imperial (Metric)

2 lemons, medium size
2 tablespoons raw cane sugar
1-1½ pints (570-850ml) boiling
   water

American

2 lemons, medium size
2 tablespoons raw cane sugar
2½-3¾ cups boiling water

1. Scrub the skins of the lemons well. Peel the rind thinly, put into a large jug with the sugar and pour over the boiling water.

2. Allow to cool, then add the juice squeezed from the lemons. Serve chilled.

LEMON AND LIME DRINK

Grain Free	Gluten Free	Milk Free	Egg Free

Choose limes that are beginning to yellow, as these are juicier than the dark green ones.

Imperial (Metric)	American
1 lemon	1 lemon
2 tablespoons raw cane sugar	2 tablespoons raw cane sugar
1½ pints (850ml) boiling water	3¾ cups boiling water
1 lime	1 lime

1. Scrub the lemon well. Peel the rind thinly, put into a large jug with the sugar, then pour over the boiling water.

2. Allow to cool, then add the juice squeezed from the lemon and the lime. Chill well before serving.

FRESH LIMEADE

Grain Free	Gluten Free	Milk Free	Egg Free

Imperial (Metric)	American
1½ pints (850ml) water	3¾ cups water
2 tablespoons raw cane sugar	2 tablespoons raw cane sugar
2 limes	2 limes

1. Heat the water in a saucepan, then stir in the sugar and mix until dissolved.

2. Allow to cool. Squeeze the juice from the limes and add to the mixture. Serve chilled.

LEMON BARLEY WATER (1)

Milk Free   Egg Free

This is a nourishing drink and ideal for illness and convalescence.

Imperial (Metric)

2 oz (55g) pot barley (not pearl barley which has had a lot of goodness removed in processing)

2 lemons, medium size (scrub skins well)

½-2 pints (850ml to 1.14 litres) water

2 tablespoons honey or raw cane sugar

American

⅓ cup pot barley (not pearl barley which has had a lot of goodness removed in processing)

2 lemons, medium size (scrub skins well)

3¾-5 cups water

2 tablespoons honey or raw cane sugar

1. Wash the barley in a sieve. Slice the lemons.

2. Put the barley, lemons and water in a saucepan and bring to the boil. Simmer for approximately 2 hours until barley is soft. (This takes approximately 5 minutes in a pressure cooker.)

3. Strain and cool. Add the honey or sugar.

LEMON BARLEY WATER (2)

Milk Free   Egg Free

Imperial (Metric)

2 oz (55g) pot barley

2 lemons, medium size (scrub skins well)

1½-2 pints (850ml to 1.14 litres) boiling water

2 tablespoons honey or raw cane sugar

American

⅓ cup pot barley

2 lemons, medium size (scrub skins well)

3¾-5 cups boiling water

2 tablespoons honey or raw cane sugar

1. Wash the barley and slice the lemons. Pour on the boiling water.

2. Cool and add the honey. Leave to stand overnight or for at least 12 hours for all the goodness to be extracted. Strain.

GINGER BEER

Grain Free	Gluten Free	Milk Free	Egg Free

Imperial (Metric)	*American*
1 lb (455g) raw cane sugar	2⅔ cups raw cane sugar
2 oz (55g) root ginger	2 ounces root ginger
6 pints (3.5 litres) water	15 cups water
1 oz (30g) cream of tartar	1½ tablespoons cream of tartar
1 lemon	1 lemon
½ oz (15g) fresh yeast or 1 teaspoon dried yeast	1¼ tablespoons fresh yeast or 1 teaspoon dried yeast

1. Boil gently the sugar and crushed root ginger with 4 pints (2.3 litres, 10 cups) of water for 10 minutes.

2. Put the remaining water into a large bowl with the cream of tartar. Pour the boiling water on to it, and add the juice of the lemon.

3. Allow to cool until it is lukewarm, then stir in the yeast. Cover with a cloth and leave to stand overnight.

4. Skim off the yeast, strain and bottle. This needs to be drunk fairly quickly or it will turn into ginger wine of sorts. Lovely for children's parties.

Note: This contains a lot of sugar so it is best kept for special occasions only.

HIBISCUS PUNCH

| Grain Free | Gluten Free | Milk Free | Egg Free |

Imperial (Metric)

2 hibiscus tea bags
½ vanilla pod
1 teaspoon cinnamon
1 pint (570ml) boiling water
1 tablespoon honey

American

2 hibiscus tea bags
½ vanilla bean
1 teaspoon cinnamon
2½ cups boiling water
1 tablespoon honey

1. Place the bags, vanilla pod (vanilla bean) and cinnamon in a saucepan.

2. Cover with the boiling water and allow to infuse for 5 minutes. Strain and add honey to taste. Serve hot in winter or cold in summer.

Note: You can add chopped pear or cubes of pineapple, with extra pineapple or pear juice to make it even better.

GLOSSARY

SALICYLATES
Aspirin sensitivity usually reveals itself as a wheeze when it is taken to relieve pain or fever, though it can also cause rashes and other allergic symptoms. Breathing problems would probably first be noticed an hour or two after taking the aspirin. People who are allergic to aspirin are usually sensitive to the 'acetyl' part of acetyl salicylic acid, though some are sensitive to all salicylates.

Natural salicylate is a substance closely allied to aspirin and which occurs naturally in certain foods. People who are sensitive to aspirin may also have a reaction to these foods.

Several synthetic flavourings used in foods contain a salicylate radical. Salicylates also crop up in chewing gum, soft and fizzy drinks, toothpastes, mouthwashes, suntan lotions, lozenges, ice creams, jams and jellies.

SALT OF BENZOIC ACID
This is a white crystalline organic acid produced commercially from petro chemicals, and used as an antiseptic and preservative, and in certain types of dyes. It occurs naturally in peas, pineapple and cranberries.

ANTIOXIDANT
This is a substance added to oils and fats to stop them going rancid when exposed to oxygen in the air. Ascorbic acid (vitamin C) and the tocopherols (vitamin E family) both have antioxidant properties.

The synthetic antioxidants B.H.A. (butylated hydroxyanisole) and B.H.T. (butylated hydroxytoluene) are widely used as antioxidants for animal fats, but for the last 20 years have been thought to be dangerous. Some research has shown that the effects on humans include asthma, dermatitis and tingling on the skin. They are found to build up in the body fat, and most people eat large amounts of these. They have been banned in many other countries, but not in Britain!

COELIAC DISEASE
A disease in which damage to the lining of the intestine prevents the body from absorbing important nutrients. Symptoms are loss of weight, diarrhoea with offensive stools full of undigested fat, stomach pain, and sometimes vomiting. These symptoms are caused by an intolerance of gluten, a protein found in wheat, barley, rye and oats. Many people with coeliac disease respond to the removal of these grains, but those more severely affected may need to eliminate other foods containing gluten-type protein.

APPENDIX I:

HYPERACTIVITY

HYPERACTIVE CHILDREN'S SUPPORT GROUP
For Hyperactive, Allergic and Learning Disabled Children.

Aims of the Group
A. The relief of children who are in need of care and attention by reason of being handicapped through hyperactivity.
B. To conduct research and promote investigation into the incidence of hyperactivity in the U.K., its causes and treatments; and to disseminate information concerning this condition.

About the Hyperactive Children's Support Group
The Hyperactive Children's Support Group was founded in November 1977 and grew into a national association almost overnight. The group was granted charitable status in May 1979, Registered Charity 277643. The Group is not in receipt of any Government Grants or Loans. The only financial support comes from members' subscriptions, outside donations and the sale of literature.

The Group supplies information on dietary therapy and other forms of help and treatment. Newsletters keep members, both lay and professional, up to date with latest research and other important data.

Hyperactive children are often allergic (intolerant of some foods and chemicals) and learning disabled because they are not able to concentrate. These children have a very short attention span even though they may be bright and intelligent (see page 228 for symptoms).

We ask for open minds on the subject of the dietary and other suggested treatment approaches to this multiple handicap as an alternative to drug based therapy. The Group cannot offer individual medical advice as NO MEMBER HAS ANY MEDICAL

QUALIFICATIONS. However, the Group has medical advisers and is in touch with various hospitals and doctors who are willing to help. Professional enquiries welcome.

For full information write to Sally Bunday, Secretary, Hyperactive Children's Support Group, 59 Meadowside, Angmering, Littlehampton, West Sussex BN16 4BW. Mark your envelope 'Information Only' and send a stamped, addressed envelope (9×4 inches, 23×10cm).

Hon. Chairman: Mrs I. D. Colquhoun

Family Membership — First year £2 + £3 for diet booklet. Annual renewal £5. This entitles members to three newsletters per year, local group contact, free advice and help.

For £3 the Group will send details of the diet, etc. Ideally it is best for parents to join as members so that they can be kept in touch with new information on 'safe foods', research projects, and many other items. If a copy of the diet only is required please send £3 and mark envelope 'Diet Please'.

SYMPTOMS AND DESCRIPTIVE CHARACTERISTICS

Not every child will have all the symptoms and these will be in varying degrees.

In Infancy

Crying, screaming, restlessness — needing very little sleep.
Colic — very difficult to feed whether breast or bottle fed.
Cannot be pacified or cuddled — often spurns affection.
Excessive dribbling — may be very thirsty.
Head banging — cot rocking.
Fits and tantrums.
May not crawl.

In Older Children (in addition to the above)

Clumsy, impulsive — often accident prone.
Erratic, disruptive behaviour.
Compulsive touching — everything and everyone.
Constant motion — wriggles legs.
May walk on toes — runs everywhere.
Disturbs other children — may be aggressive.
Unable to concentrate — never finish anything they begin.

Demands must be met immediately. Frustration leads to temper tantrums. Normal or high I.Q. but fails at school.
Poor appetite — poor hand and eye co-ordination.
Uncooperative — defiant and disobedient.
Self-abusive (pulling hair/picking skin, etc.)
Continued problems with sleep — wakes many times in the night. Cannot sit through a meal.
Many hyperactive children also suffer speech, hearing, vision and memory defects.
Other health problems include infantile colic, eczema, asthma, hay fever, rhinitis, and repeated chest and ear infections.

DETAILS OF DIET

This cookery book is based on the 'food programme' formulated by the late Dr Ben Feingold M.D., an American allergist, who spent many years researching the possibility of chemical food additives being linked to hyperactivity and behavioural disturbances. His aim was to get children better without causing harm — i.e. using diet in the management of hyperactivity as an alternative to drugs.

Two groups of food are eliminated by this diet.

Group 1.
All food and drink containing synthetic COLOURING and FLAVOURING are forbidden. Also Monosodium Glutamate, Sodium Glutamate, Nitrite, Nitrate, Butylated Hydroxytoluene (B.H.T.), Butylated Hydroxyanisole (B.H.A.) used as antioxidants, sodium benzoate, benzoic acid.

Group 2.
Certain fruits and vegetables containing naturally occurring 'salicylates' to which these children may be sensitive. (See glossary on salicylates.)

Not Permitted

Almonds
Apples (also cider and cider vinegar)
Apricots
All berries (Bilberries, blackberries, boysenberries, strawberries,

raspberries, gooseberries, elderberries, and dewberries)
Cherries
Cloves
Coffee
Cucumbers and gherkins
Currants, grapes and raisins (also wine and wine vinegar)
All peppers and chillies
Nectarines
Oranges
Peaches
Plums and prunes
Tangerines
Teas
Tomatoes
Oil of Wintergreen

Because of the elimination of these fruit and vegetables, it is important for the children to get sufficient vitamin C and although there are many other sources in the permitted fruit and vegetables as listed below the Group can advise on extra vitamin supplements.

Permitted Fruit

Avocados
Bananas
Dates
Figs
Grapefruit
Guavas
Lemons
Limes
Loquats

Mangoes
All melons
Papaya
Pears
Persimmon (Sharon fruit)
Pineapple
Pomegranate
Pumpkin
Rhubarb

Permitted Vegetables

Alfalfa sprouts
Artichokes
Asparagus
Aubergine (eggplant)

Kale
Kohlrabi
Lettuce
Lentils

Beans (all types)
Bean sprouts
Beetroot (beets)
Broccoli
Brussels sprouts
Cabbage
Calabrese
Cauliflower
Celery
Celeriac
Chard
Chicory
Chinese leaves
Chives
Cress
Collard Greens
Courgettes (zucchini)
Endive
Fennel

Marrow (summer squash)
Okra
Olives
Onions
Parsley
Parsnip
Peas
Potatoes
Radish (red and white)
Sorrel
Spinach
Spring greens
Spring onions (scallions)
Squash
Swede (rutabaga)
Sweetcorn (sweetcorn kernel)
Sweet potato
Turnip
Watercress

Permitted

All seeds and nuts *except* Almonds

Pulses
(Whole not split are best)

Aduki beans
Black eye beans
Butter beans (Lima beans)
Canellini beans
Chickpeas (garbanzo beans)
Flageolet beans
Haricot beans (navy beans)
Kidney beans
Lentils
Mung beans
Borlotti beans (pinto beans)
Soya beans (soy beans)

In cases of extreme salicylate sensitivity Dr Feingold recommended the elimination of other salicylate-containing foods, these being potatoes, bananas, coffee, pineapple, and all sources of benzoates (see Glossary). Benzoate occurs naturally in cranberries and peas and is also used frequently as a preservative e.g. sodium benzoate, benzoate of soda, etc. Other salicylate-containing fruits not on the Feingold list are tamarind, passion fruit, olive, peppermint and mint.

Despite extensive enquiries it is proving difficult to ascertain accurate details on amounts of salicylates contained in foods. You may need to test each fruit and vegetable separately.

The willow tree was the original source of pain-killing medicines made from salicylates and the leaves, bark, fruits, flowers and stems of willow and the following plants contain salicylates:

acacia
aspen
birch
calcanthus
camelia
hyacinth
marigold
milkwort
poplar
spirea
teaberry
tulip
violet

OTHER FACTORS AFFECTING HYPERACTIVITY
There are a number of chemical or environmental hazards which may also affect you or your child.

In the Home

1.   Aerosols, such as spray polishes, window, pan, oven or shoe cleaners.
2.   Insecticides.
3.   Felt tipped pens.
4.   Newsprint.

5. Solid air fresheners.
6. Perfumes, hair sprays, coloured bubble baths and toothpastes.
7. Avoid synthetic fabrics, such as polyester. Natural fabrics are better. Be wary of dry cleaning, waterproofing and moth-proofing etc.
8. Washing powders, particularly the types containing enzymes. Clothes washed in any detergent should be well rinsed. Some can cause severe irritation and eczema.
9. Washing up liquid. Dishes should be rinsed in hot water.
10. Paint and varnish fumes.
11. Natural gas, coal fires and paraffin heaters may affect some children.
12. Animal fur.
13. House dust.
14. Tap water. This contains chlorine, and possibly fluoride which may affect some children and adults. We suggest you try filtered or bottled water for drinking and cooking. See page 262 for water filter.

Environmental Hazards

1. Swimming baths. The chlorine affects many children, particularly hyperactive ones.
2. Diesel fumes, petrol fumes, formaldehyde fumes from modern furnishings and carpets.
3. Glues and other industrial solvents.
4. Foods. Apart from the artificial colourings, flavourings, preservatives, etc., which are added to our foods, many poisonous sprays, insecticides and herbicides are put on to it while it is growing. Chemicals are also sprayed on to fruit to prevent it from ripening too soon, or it can be dyed to make it look riper than it is.
5. Many farm animals are raised in factory conditions. Antibiotics are added to their feeds and some cattle are given growth hormones. Residues of these are left in these foods, which we then eat.

6. Heavy metals
   a) *Lead*. This is extremely toxic and affects the nervous system. Children and the unborn child are particularly susceptible.
   Sources
   1. Petrol.
   2. Old paint. Children may chew this. Avoid dry sanding old lead paint, as the lead can be inhaled.
   3. Lead solder from tins (cans) — the lead can get into the food.
   4. Drinking water. Leached from old lead pipes, more likely in soft water areas.
   5. Road dust.
   b) *Cadmium* — from cigarette smoking, or inhaling smoke while someone is smoking.
   c) *Aluminium*
   1. Aluminium saucepans and foil cooking containers.
   2. Some baking powders.
   3. Deodorants.

Toxic levels of lead, cadmium, aluminium and copper, or deficiencies of essential minerals such as calcium, iron, magnesium and zinc can have an adverse affect on health and can increase hyperactivity. Hair metal analysis tests are useful for obtaining an indication of your trace metal status.

Caution: Any supplements needed as a result of these tests must be prescribed by a qualified doctor in this field. Full details from the Hyperactive Children's Support Group, at the address on page 228.

FOOD ALLERGIES OR INTOLERANCES
The following are some likely foods which may cause reaction:

Cow's milk	Corn
Grains	Coffee
Sugar	Yeast
Eggs	Rye
Chocolate	Malt
Cheese	Beef (if intolerant to milk)
Pork	

A rotation diet will help to track these down.

WARNING. If you suspect your child is allergic to cow's milk, it is essential to seek medical advice. Once a child is taken off cow's milk it is very dangerous to put a child back on it again, especially infants.

Sedatives — Sedatives can have a reverse affect on hyperactive children. Ask your physician or pharmacist to prescribe non-coloured, non-flavoured drugs and medicines.

All the following products are available at health food stores. Remember to read all labels carefully.

GRAIN FREE FLOURS

CHICK PEA (GARBANZO) FLOUR. Also known as besan or gram flour.
LIMA BEAN FLOUR. Also known as butter bean, curry bean or pole bean.
LENTIL FLOUR
POTATO FLOUR. Also known as potato farina.
SOYA (SOY) FLOUR
SPLIT PEA FLOUR

ARROWROOT Although safe for a grain free diet, arrowroot, sago,
SAGO   and tapioca are starches and supply only empty
TAPIOCA   calories. It is better to use the above flours.

A THICKENING AGENT. Use soya (soy), Lima or potato flour for savoury dishes and agar agar, which is high in minerals, for sweet foods. Chick pea flour is quite sweet and is good in cakes.

GLUTEN FREE FLOURS

Gluten is a substance found in wheat, rye, barley and oats. People with coeliac disease cannot absorb the protein gluten in these grains. However some people with a wheat intolerance may be able to tolerate oats and barley, while others can tolerate wheat if it has been organically grown ie. not treated with pesticides. Grains that may be used as flours are:
MAIZE (CORNMEAL). Also known as corn.
MILLET
RICE
BUCKWHEAT
Also any of the grain free flours listed above.

MILK FREE DIETS

Use a milk free margarine.

Use water instead of milk or use soya (soy) milk products (see page 237) or nut milks (see page 36).

Avoid

BUTTER

MARGARINE

CHEESE (This may be tolerated by some, especially when made with vegetable rennet and not calf rennet).

CREAM

MILK (Goat's or sheep's milk may be tolerated).

YOGURT (This may be tolerated).

EGG FREE DIETS

Egg replacer is available at health food stores and from Foodwatch (see page 256).

IMPORTANT NOTES

1. The flours for grain free and gluten free diets are interchangeable to suit individual tastes and allergies concerned. Soya (soy) flour (unless allergic to it) should be included to make sure you are getting a balanced protein intake.

2. Cornflour increases gastric acidity as opposed to maizemeal (cornmeal). Cantassium produce a guaranteed gluten free maize meal.

3. Information and recipes regarding grain free, gluten free, milk free and egg free diets are merely a guide to those who must follow these diets. Full medical help is essential and must be followed. With this in mind we hope these recipes prove helpful. For further reading on allergies see Recommended Reading on page 266.

4. The codings at the top of each recipe will help you find your requirements quickly.

5. REMEMBER

   We are all individuals, so certain foods which claim to be safe for certain diets may not be tolerated by you!!

SOYA (SOY) PRODUCTS

Soya (Soy) Beans contain as much protein as top quality steak, the difference being that they contain unsaturated fat, as well as all eight essential amino acids which the body cannot manufacture. Therefore the soya (soy) bean is a complete protein, highest in nutritional value of all beans. The whole beans take longer to cook than most although a pressure cooker reduces the time to 25-30 minutes. As with all beans they must be thoroughly cooked. For cooking times see page 61.

Soya (Soy) Flour is best bought pre-cooked. It may be added to soups, casseroles and gravies as a thickening agent and to make a protein balanced meal. Soyolk is a natural full fibre pre-cooked full fat flour.

Tofu or soya (soy) bean curd is a high quality, low cost protein, free of cholesterol and high in polyunsaturated fats. Can be a key ingredient in many recipes such as spreads, soups, egg, vegetable and grain dishes.
Caution — the coagulant used in Morinaga tofu is prepared from corn starch by a fermentation process. This may cause a reaction in corn 'sensitive' people.

Soya (Soy) Milk can be obtained in cans, cartons or spray dried milk powder. Suitable for infant feeding, but read labels carefully on this. It is richer in iron than cow's milk but has less calcium, phosphorus and vitamin A. Plamil manufacture a soya (soy) bean plant milk. It is formulated from natural ingredients and includes sunflower oil, calcium, phosphorus and lecithin. Also available carob (chocolate substitute) flavoured.

Soya (Soy) Cream. Plamil Delice is a substitute for dairy cream and is rich in polyunsaturates.

Soya (Soy) Sauce Tamari is a natural soya (soy) sauce which contains little or no wheat. Use as a seasoning and to bring out the flavour in gravies, soups, sauces, casseroles and stews.

Shoyu. A natural soya (soy) sauce which contains soya (soy) beans and wheat. Use as for tamari.

Miso. This is fermented soya (soy) bean in paste form. Use as for soya (soy) sauce. A marvellous health giving food, very good for soups.

ESSENTIAL FATTY ACIDS

The essential fatty acids are linoleic and alpha linolenic acid. They are called essential as they cannot be manufactured by the body. These fatty acids are found in vegetable and seed oils particularly safflower, sunflower and corn oil. Although expensive, cold pressed oils are better as these have not been heated during refining.

Studies suggest that a number of hyperactive and allergic children may be unable to metabolise essential fatty acids because of inhibited enzyme activity (which may occur through faulty diet or illness), or lack of sufficient linoleic acid in the diet or the necessary co-factors (zinc, magnesium, B vitamins and vitamin C) needed for the conversion of linoleic acid to Prostaglandin E.1.

Prostaglandin E.1. appears to be important in the control of the immune system — behaviour — kidneys — thirst — asthma — eczema. Many hyperactive children appear to suffer from excessive thirst and have low levels of zinc.

For more information on essential fatty acids as a supplement, research paper and parents' notes write to the Secretary, H.A.C.S.G. at the address on page 228. Please send 30p in stamps and an 8×10 inch stamped addressed envelope.

APPENDIX II:

SPECIAL DIETS

IDEAS FOR GRAIN FREE AND MILK FREE MEALS

BREAKFAST
Honey Cinnamon Grapefruit.
Grapefruit and Melon Refresher.
Soya (Soy) Yogurt.
Hazelnut Milk Shake.
Delicious Seed Milk.
Cashew Nut Milk.

SOUPS
Everything Soup.
Carrot and Lemon Soup.
Watercress Soup.
Leek and Potato Soup.

MAIN MEALS (Note: Beef may be a problem for those allergic to milk)
Beef and Swede (Rutabaga) Loaf.
Beef and Bean Curry.
Roast Lamb with Garlic and Rosemary.
Shish Kebab.
Grain Free Dumplings.
Lemon Chicken.
Carrot and Potato Flour Loaf.
Special Savoury Lentils.
Dhal.
Chickpea (Garbanzo Bean) and Haricot (Navy Bean) Bake.
Homemade Tofu.
Beefburgers (Hamburgers).
Mushroom Beefburgers (Hamburgers).

SALADS
Bean Salad.
Carrot Salad.
Beansprout and Cashew Nut Salad.
Beetroot (Beet) Medley.
Beetroot (Beet) Salad.
Green Salad.
Melon and Prawn Salad.
Cauliflower Salad.
Coleslaw.
Mayonnaise.
Mushroom Mayonnaise.
Mayonnaise without vinegar.

PUDDINGS
Dried fruits and jellied fruits.
Fresh Fruit Salad.
Mango Tofu Surprise.
Soya (Soy) Crumble.
Spiced Rhubarb Jelly.
Baked Marzipan Pears.
Banana Sweet.
Instant Lemon Pudding.
Pineapple Jelly.
Lemon Sauce.
Custard/Milk Pudding.
Magic Cream.
Nut Cream.
Tofu Whipped Cream.
Basic Sponge/Pudding (recipe under bread and cake section)

BREAD AND CAKES
Potato Bread Yeast Free.
Basic Sponge/Pudding recipe.
Coconut Pyramids.
Hazelnut Macaroons.
Mincemeat.
Citrus Peel for Cakes and Puddings.

Marzipan.
No Sugar Icing.
Butter Cream Filling or Topping.

SPREADS
Peanut Butter.
Vegetarian Pâté.
Hummus.
Vegetable Cream Cheese.
Pear Blender.

SANDWICH FILLINGS
See section.

JAMS AND CHUTNEYS
See section.

SWEETS, PARTIES, SPECIAL OCCASIONS
Sesame Dip.
Avocado Dip
Crispy Spicy Nuts.
Guava Lime Ice Cream.
Tropical Pineapple Fruit Salad.
Iced Lollies (Popsicles).
Sunflower/Sesame Bars.
Honey Halva.

DRINKS
See section, or general index.

IDEAS FOR GRAIN FREE MEALS

BREAKFASTS
Honey Cinnamon Grapefruit.
Grapefruit and Melon Refresher.
Fruity Breakfast Yogurt.
Yogurt.
Soya (Soy) Yogurt.
Banana and Lemon Health Drink.
Hazelnut Milk Shake.
Delicious Seed Milk.
Cashew Nut Milk.

SOUPS
Everything Soup.
Cauliflower Soup.
Bortsch.
Carrot and Lemon Soup.
Watercress Soup.
Leek and Potato Soup.

MAIN MEALS
Beef and Swede (Rutabaga) Loaf.
Beef and Bean Curry.
Roast Lamb with Garlic and Rosemary.
Lemon Lamb Meatballs.
Shish Kebab.
Grain Free Dumplings.
Lemon Chicken.
Cauliflower and Butter Bean (Lima Bean) Curry.
Carrot and Potato Flour Loaf.
Brussels Sprouts with Chestnuts.
Special Savoury Lentils.
Dhal.
Lentil Roast.
Chickpea (Garbanzo Bean) and Haricot (Navy Bean) Bake.
Homemade Tofu (recipe under Spreads)
Beefburgers (Hamburgers).
Mushroom Beefburgers (Hamburgers).

SALADS
Banana Salad.
Bean Salad.
Carrot Salad.
Beansprout and Cashew Nut Salad.
Green Salad.
Beetroot (Beet) Medley.
Beetroot (Beet) Salad.
Red Cabbage Caraway.
Melon and Prawn Salad.
Melon Ginger and Curd Cheese Salad.
Cauliflower Salad.

Coleslaw.
Mayonnaise.
Mushroom Mayonnaise.
Mayonnaise without vinegar.

PUDDINGS
Dried Fruits and Jellied Fruits.
Fresh Fruit Salad.
Fig and Yogurt Dessert.
Mango Tofu Surprise.
Soya (Soy) Crumble.
Rhubarb Fool.
Spiced Rhubarb Jelly.
Baked Marzipan Pears.
Banana Sweet.
Butterscotch Bananas.
Instant Lemon Pudding.
Chestnut Delight.
Pineapple Cream.
Pineapple Jelly.
Junket.
Baked Custard.
Caramel Custard.
Lemon Sauce.
Custard Sauce.
Custard/Milk Pudding.
Magic Cream.
Nut Cream.
Tofu Whipped Cream.
Yogurt Ice Cream.
Carob Ice Cream.
Basic Sponge/Pudding (recipe under bread and cake section).

BREAD AND CAKES
Potato Bread Yeast Free.
Basic Sponge/Pudding Recipe.
Coconut Pyramids.
Mincemeat.

Citrus Peel for Cakes and Puddings.
Marzipan.
No Sugar Icing.
Fudge Icing.
Carob Yogurt Filling.
Butter Cream Filling or Topping.

SPREADS
Peanut Butter.
Vegetarian Pâté.
Hummus.
Vegetable Cream Cheese.
Pear Blender.

SANDWICH FILLINGS
See section.

JAMS AND CHUTNEYS
See section.

SWEETS, PARTIES, SPECIAL OCCASIONS
Sesame Dip.
Quark Dip.
Avocado Dip.
Crispy Spicy Nuts.
Guava Lime Ice Cream.
Tropical Pineapple Fruit Salad.
Iced Lollies (Popsicles).
Sunflower/Sesame Bars.
Honey Halva.
Toffee.
Toffee Pears.
Homemade Carob Easter Eggs.

DRINKS
See section, or general index.

IDEAS FOR GLUTEN FREE MEALS

BREAKFASTS
Honey Cinnamon Grapefruit.
Grapefruit and Melon Refresher.
Fruity Breakfast Yogurt.
Yogurt.
Soya (Soy) Yogurt.
Millet Porridge.
Salmon Kedgeree.
Banana and Lemon Health Drink.
Hazelnut Milk Shake.
Delicious Seed Milk.
Cashew Nut Milk.

SOUPS
Everything Soup.
Cauliflower Soup.
Minestrone.
Bortsch.
Carrot and Lemon Soup.
Watercress Soup.
Leek and Potato Soup.

MAIN MEALS
Beef and Swede (Rutabaga) Loaf.
Beef and Bean Curry.
Roast Lamb with Garlic and Rosemary.
Lemon Lamb Meatballs.
Shish Kebabs.
Grain Free Dumplings.
Lemon Chicken.
Cauliflower and Butter Bean (Lima Bean) Curry.
Courgette (Zucchini) Mornay.
Rice and Cheese Savoury.
Sweetcorn and Mushroom Bake.
Chinese Rice.
Stir Fry Vegetables in a Sweet & Sour Sauce.
Vegetable Crumble.

Carrot and Potato Flour Loaf.
Brussels Sprouts with Chestnuts.
Special Savoury Lentils.
Dahl.
Lentil Roast.
Black Eye Bean Loaf.
Chickpea (Garbanzo Bean) and Haricot (Navy Bean) Bake.
Homemade Tofu (recipe under Spreads).
Beefburgers (Hamburgers).
Mushroom Beefburgers (Hamburgers).
Brown Rice Cheeseburgers.
Nut and Millet Rissoles.

SALADS
Banana Salad.
Rice Salad.
Bean Salad.
Carrot Salad.
Beansprout and Cashew Nut Salad.
Green Salad.
Beetroot (Beet) Medley.
Beetroot (Beet) Salad.
Red Cabbage Caraway.
Melon and Prawn Salad.
Melon, Ginger and Curd Cheese Salad.
Cauliflower Salad.
Coleslaw.
Mayonnaise.
Mushroom Mayonnaise.
Mayonnaise without vinegar.

PUDDINGS
Dried Fruits and Jellied Fruits.
Fresh Fruit Salad.
Fig and Yogurt Dessert.
Mango Tofu Surprise.
Soya (Soy) Crumble.
Rhubarb Fool.

Spiced Rhubarb Jelly.
Baked Marzipan Pears.
Pear 'Clafoutis'.
Banana Sweet.
Butterscotch Bananas.
Coconut Supreme.
Lime Mousse.
Instant Lemon Pudding.
Chestnut Delight.
Pineapple Cream.
Pineapple Meringue Pudding.
Pineapple Jelly.
Junket.
Millet Milk Pudding.
Baked Custard.
Caramel Custard.
Lemon Sauce.
Custard Sauce.
Custard/Milk Pudding.
Magic Cream.
Nut Cream.
Tofu Whipped Cream.
Yogurt Ice Cream.
Carob Ice Cream.
Basic Sponge/Pudding (recipe under Bread and Cakes).

BREAD, CAKES AND PASTRY
Potato Bread Yeast Free.
Gluten Free Bread.
Gluten Free Pastry.
Gluten Free Biscuits.
Chickpea (Garbanzo Bean)/Rice Flour Crispbreads.
Cinnamon and Ginger Cake with Sticky Lemon Topping.
Basic Sponge/Pudding Recipe.
Coconut Pyramids.
Hazelnut Macaroons.
Mincemeat.
Citrus Peel for Cakes and Puddings.

Marzipan.
No Sugar Icing.
Fudge Icing.
Carob Yogurt Filling.
Butter Filling or Topping.

SPREADS
Peanut Butter.
Vegetarian Pâté.
Hummus.
Vegetable Cream Cheese.
Pear Blender.

SANDWICH FILLINGS
See section.

JAMS AND CHUTNEYS
See section.

SWEETS, PARTIES AND SPECIAL OCCASIONS
Sesame Dip.
Quark Dip.
Avocado Dip.
Crispy Spicy Nuts.
Pineapple and Ginger Macaroon Gateau.
Profiteroles with Carob Sauce.
Guava Lime Ice Cream.
Tropical Pineapple Fruit Salad.
Iced Lollies (Popsicles).
Sunflower/Sesame Bars.
Fruit Bars.
Pop Corn.
Honey Halva.
Toffee.
Toffee Pears.
Homemade Carob Easter Eggs.

DRINKS
See section or general index.

IDEAS FOR MILK FREE MEALS

BREAKFASTS
Honey Cinnamon Grapefruit.
Grapefruit and Melon Refresher.
Crunchy Muesli with Soya (Soy) Milk.
Soya (Soy) Yogurt.
Oatmeal Porridge.
Millet Porridge with Soya (Soy) Milk.
Salmon Kedgeree.
Hazelnut Milk Shake.
Delicious Seed Milk
Cashew Nut Milk.

SOUPS
Everything Soup.
Minestrone.
Carrot and Lemon Soup.
Watercress Soup.
Leek and Potato Soup.

MAIN MEALS
Casserole of Beef.
Beef and Swede (Rutabaga) Loaf.
Beef and Bean Curry.
Roast Lamb with Garlic and Rosemary.
Shish Kebab.
Grain Free Dumplings.
Liver Lyonnaise.
Lemon Chicken.
Fish Fingers (Sticks).
Cauliflower Fritters.
Chinese Rice.
Stir Fry Vegetables in Sweet and Sour Sauce.
Vegetable Crumble.
Carrot and Potato Flour Loaf.
Celebration Nut Roast.
Chestnut Stuffing/Loaf.
Special Savoury Lentils.

Dhal.
Black Eye Bean Loaf.
Chickpea (Garbanzo Bean) and Haricot (Navy Bean) Bake.
Baked Beans.
Homemade Tofu (recipe under Spreads).
Beefburgers (Hamburgers).
Mushroom Beefburgers (Hamburgers).
Nut and Millet Rissoles.

SALADS
Rice Salad.
Bean Salad.
Carrot Salad.
Beansprout and Cashew Nut Salad.
Green Salad.
Beetroot (Beet) Medley.
Beetroot (Beet) Salad.
Melon and Prawn Salad.
Cauliflower Salad.
Coleslaw.
Homemade Salad Cream.
French Dressing.
Mayonnaise.
Mushroom Mayonnaise.
Mayonnaise without vinegar.

PUDDINGS
Dried Fruits and Jellied Fruits.
Fresh Fruit Salad.
Mango Tofu Surprise.
Soya (Soy) Crumble.
Spiced Rhubarb Jelly.
Baked Marzipan Pears.
Carob Pear Pudding.
Banana Sweet.
Lime Mousse.
Instant Lemon Pudding.
Pineapple Jelly.

Lemon Sauce.
Custard/Milk Pudding.
Magic Cream.
Nut Cream.
Tofu Whipped Cream.
Basic Sponge/Pudding (recipe under Bread and Cake section)

BREADS AND CAKES
Potato Bread Yeast Free.
Homemade Wholemeal Bread.
Chickpea (Garbanzo Bean)/Rice Flour Crispbread.
Basic Sponge/Pudding Recipe.
Coconut Pyramids.
Hazelnut Macaroons.
Crunchie Cookies.
Cannon Balls.
Christmas Pudding.
Mincemeat.
Citrus Peel for cakes and puddings.
Marzipan.
No Sugar Icing.
Butter Cream Filling or Topping.

SPREADS
Peanut Butter.
Vegetarian Pâté.
Hummus.
Vegetable Cream Cheese.
Pear Blender.

SANDWICH FILLINGS
See section.

JAMS AND CHUTNEYS
See section.

SWEETS, PARTIES AND SPECIAL OCCASIONS
Sesame Dip.
Avocado Dip.

Crispy Spicy Nuts.
Guava Lime Ice Cream.
Tropical Pineapple Fruit Salad.
Iced Lollies (Popsicles).
Sunflower/Sesame Bars.
Fruit Bars.
Pop Corn.
Honey Halva.

DRINKS
See section, or general index.

IDEAS FOR EGG FREE MEALS

BREAKFASTS
Honey Cinnamon Grapefruit.
Grapefruit and Melon Refresher.
Alpine Breakfast.
Crunchy Muesli.
Cinnamon Toast.
Fruity Breakfast Yogurt.
Yogurt.
Soya (Soy) Yogurt.
Oatmeal Porridge.
Millet Porridge.
Parsnip or Swede (Rutabaga) Fritters.
Herrings in Oatmeal.
Oatcakes.
Dried Fruit Shake.
Banana and Lemon Health Drink.
Hazelnut Shake.
Delicious Seed Milk.
Cashew Nut Milk.

SOUPS
Everything Soup.
Cauliflower Soup.
Minestrone.
Bortsch.

Carrot and Lemon Soup.
Watercress Soup.
Leek and Potato Soup.

MAIN MEALS
Casserole of Beef.
Beef and Bean Curry.
Roast Lamb with Garlic and Rosemary.
Lemon Lamb Meatballs.
Shish Kebab.
Dumplings.
Liver Lyonnaise.
Lemon Chicken.
Cauliflower, and Butter Bean (Lima Bean) Curry.
Baked Fish in Yogurt Sauce.
Courgette (Zucchini) Mornay.
Stir Fry Vegetables in Sweet and Sour Sauce.
Sweetcorn and Mushroom Bake.
Vegetable Crumble.
Brussels Sprouts with Chestnuts.
Special Savoury Lentils.
Dahl.
Black Eye Bean Loaf.
Chickpea (Garbanzo Bean) and Haricot (Navy Bean) Bake.
Baked Beans.
Homemade Tofu (recipe under Spreads).
Beefburgers.

SALADS
Rice Salad.
Bean Salad.
Carrot Salad.
Beansprout and Cashew Nut Salad.
Green Salad.
Beetroot (Beet) Medley.
Red Cabbage Caraway.
Melon, Ginger and Curd Cheese Salad.
French Dressing.

PUDDINGS
Dried Fruits and Jellied Fruits.
Fresh Fruit Salad.
Fig and Yogurt Dessert.
Soya (Soy) Crumble.
Mango Tofu Surprise.
Pear and Fig Oatmeal Crumble.
Date and Nut Slice.
Spiced Rhubarb Jelly.
Banana Sweet.
Butterscotch Bananas.
Pineapple Cream.
Pineapple Jelly.
Junket.
Lemon Sauce.
Millet Milk Pudding.
Nut Cream.
Tofu Whipped Cream.
Yogurt Ice Cream.
Carob Ice Cream.

BREADS, CAKES AND PASTRY
Homemade Wholemeal Bread.
Shortcrust Pastry.
Chickpea (Garbanzo Bean)/Rice Flour Crispbreads.
Sesame Thins.
Yogurt Scones.
Carob Bars.
Flapjacks.
Oat Crunchies.
Crunchie Cookies.
Cannon Balls.
Gingerbread Men.
Lemon Shortbread.
Celebration Shortbread.
Mincemeat.
Citrus peel for Cakes and Puddings.

Marzipan.
No Sugar Icing.
Fudge Icing.
Carob Yogurt Filling.
Butter Cream Filling or Topping.

SPREADS
Peanut Butter.
Hummus.
Vegetable Cream Cheese.
Pear Blender.

SANDWICH FILLINGS
See section.

JAMS AND CHUTNEYS
See section.

SWEETS, PARTIES AND SPECIAL OCCASIONS
Sesame Dip.
Quark Dip.
Avocado Dip.
Savoury Sesame Sticks.
Tropical Pineapple Fruit Salad.
Iced Lollies (Popsicles).
Wheatflake Cracklets.
Sunflower Sesame Bars.
Fruity Carob Crunch.
Fruit Bars.
Pop Corn.
Honey Halva.
Toffee.
Toffee Pears.
Homemade Carob Easter Eggs.

DRINKS
See section or general index.

APPENDIX III:

USEFUL ADDRESSES

The products listed in this section are a few of the many 'pure' foods available. A keen eye reading labels will uncover many more. All products are based on natural principles and contain no artificial additives. Correct at the time of going to press. No liability will be accepted for manufacturers' ingredient changes.

Most supermarkets, chemists or health food stores stock the items listed in this book.

Dietary Problems

Foodwatch, Butts Pond Industrial Estate, Sturminster Newton, Dorset DT10 1AZ supply pure foods especially tailored to the needs of people with special food requirements. They also have available an E.E.C. additive number list. Send s.a.e. plus 15p for further information.

The Cantassium Company produce a whole range of products especially for dietary problems. Products include vitamin and mineral supplements, and wheat free and gluten free flours.

Trufree products are available on prescription. These include Trufree Canterbread Mix, Trufree Self-Raising Flour, Breadmix with Rice Bran which behave like conventional flours. For full details write to The Cantassium Company, Larkhall Laboratories, 225-229 Putney Bridge Road, London, SW15 2PY.

LIST OF SUPPLIERS

81%-100% Wheatmeal and Wholemeal Flours	W Jordan (Cereals) Ltd, Holme Mills, Biggleswade, Bedfordshire. W. & H. Marriage & Sons Ltd, Chelmer Mills, New Street, Chelmsford, Essex CM1 1PN. Prewett's, Healthways House, 45 Station Approach, West Byfleet, Surrey KT14 6NE.
Brown Rice Flour	Harmony Foods Ltd, Cobbold Road, London. Foodwatch, Butts Pond Industrial Estate, Sturminster Newton, Dorset DT10 1AZ.
Maize Flour (meal)	The Cantassium Company, Larkhall Laboratories, 225-229 Putney Bridge Road, London SW15 2PY.
Soya (Soy) Flour	Soya Foods Ltd, New Malden House, 1 Blagdon Road, New Malden, Surrey KT3 4TB. Foodwatch (as above). Prewetts (as above).
Wheat Free and Gluten Free Baking Powder	Available at health food stores or The Cantassium Company (as above). Foodwatch (as above).
Egg Replacer	Health food stores. Foodwatch (as above).
Breakfast Cereal Grains Prewett's Wholewheat Flakes Prewett's Natural Wheat Bran Prewett's Muesli Base Prewett's Golden Grains	Prewett's (as above).

Jordans Original Crunchy (without almonds)	W. Jordan (Cereals) Ltd (as above).
Höfels Breakfast Oatflakes	Höfels Pure Food Ltd, Old
Höfels Oatmeal	Stowmarket Road, Woolpit, Bury St
Höfels Mixed Cereal	Edmunds, Suffolk IP30 9QS.
Muesli Base	
Höfels Toasted Soya Flakes	
Also other products which are either untreated or organically grown.	
Zwicky Millet Flakes	Health food stores.
100% natural, gluten free, low sodium	Swiss Mills, E. Zwicky Ltd, Mulheim, Wigoltingen, Switzerland. Distributed by Brewhurst Health Food Supplies, Byfleet, Surrey.
Yogurt	Loseley Park Farms make a full range of dairy products. Open to the public from June-September. For full details write to Loseley Park Farms, Guildford, Surrey GU3 1HN.
Vegetable Margarines, Milk Free Margarines, Fats and Oils	Health food stores. Foodwatch (as above).
Vitaquell and Vitaseig	Fauser Vitaquell, KG (GmbH and Co), Postfach 540629 D 2000 Hamburg 54 Germany.
Granose Sunflower Margarine (Milk Free)	Granose Foods Ltd, Stanborough Park, Watford, Herts. WD2 6JR.
Vegetable, nut and seed oils	Alfonal, Byfleet, Surrey. Sunwheel Foods Ltd, Granary House, Wetmore Road, Burton-on-Trent, Staffordshire.
Mapletons Suenut and Nutter Vegetable Fats	Mapletons Foods Ltd, Moss Street, Garston, Liverpool L19 2NA.

Meat
Additive-free meat
supplied by:

The Real Meat Co.
East Hill Farm
Heykesbury, Warminster, Wilts.

*Soya (Soy) Milk and Cream
Substitutes*
Plamil Soya (Soy) Plant
Milk with or without raw
cane sugar
Plamil Carob-ean —
Carob flavoured soya
(soy) plant milk
Plamil Delice — a cream
substitute
Will send details of
products, recipes and
nutritional data on infant
feeding. Write to:

Plamil Foods Ltd, Plamil House,
Bowles Well Gardens, Folkestone,
Kent. S.A.E. please.

Soya (Soy) Milk, Sugar
Free

Provamel, N.V. Alpro Protein
Products, Zuidkaai, 33B-8700
Belgium.

Formula S. Soya Food.
For infants, children
and adults
Sojal soya (soy) milk,
sugar free

Cow and Gate Ltd.
Trowbridge, Wiltshire
BA14 8YX
Hera, Haldane Foods Ltd, East
Goscote, Leicester LE4 8XJ.

Tofu

Cauldron Foods, 4 Conduit Place,
Bristol BS2 9RL. 0272-554780

Soya Ice Cream
Vanilla
Hazelnut
Plain Soya Yogurt
Soya Milk

Soya Health Foods, Unit 4,
Guinness Road, Trafford Place,
Manchester M17 1AU
061-872 0549.

Spreads

Harmony Peanut Butter
Harmony Sesame
Spread (Whole tahini)

Harmony Foods Ltd. (as above).

Sunwheel Sesame
Spread
Sunwheel Sunflower
Spread
Sunwheel Peanut Butter

Sunwheel Foods, Granary House,
Wetmore Road, Burton-on-Trent,
Staffs. DE14 1TE.

Yeast Extract

Granose Tastex

Granose Foods Ltd (as above).

Marmite

Bovril Ltd, P.O. Box 18, Wellington
Road, Burton-on-Trent, Staffordshire
DE14 2AB.

Natex Savoury Spread

Modern Health Products Ltd,
Chessington, Surrey KT9 1TH.

Savouries

Granose Sausalatas —
vegetable protein
sausages in brine

Granose Foods Ltd (as above).

Mapletons Savourmix for
making rissoles, burgers,
etc.

Mapletons Foods Ltd (as above).

Natural casings for home
sausage making and
recipes — entirely natural
casings without additives
of any kind. Write to:

Gysin and Hanson Ltd, 96 Trundleys
Road, Deptford, London SE8 5JG.

Hugli French Onion
Soup Mix

Health & Diet Food Co. Ltd,
Seymour House, 79-81 High Street,
Godalming, Surrey GU7 1BZ.

Sea Salt

Maldon Sea Salt

Maldon Crystal Salt Co. Ltd, The
Downs, Maldon, Essex CM9 7HR.

Höfels Sesame Sea Salt

Höfels Pure Food Ltd (as above).

Salt Substitute

Ruthmol low sodium condiment and cooking aid — The Cantassium Company (as above).

Miscellaneous

Taylors English Mustard, ready made without additives — Taylors Mustard Ltd, Newport Pagnell, England.

Lotus Vegetable Rennet— two types, one for making junket and one for making cheese. — Lotus Foods Ltd, Unit 3, 68 Upper Richmond Road, London SW15.

Agar Agar — gelling agent, a natural substitute for gelatine — Mapletons Foods Ltd (as above).

Gelatine — preservative free — Available from Foodwatch (as above).

Solaray Flavour Oils — claim to be 100% natural flavourings — Available from Dietmart, Unit 18, Goldsworth Park Trading Estate, Woking, Surrey.

Sugar

Billingtons Natural Unrefined Golden Granulated Sugar — Edward Billington (Sugar) Ltd, Cunard Building, Liverpool L3 1EL.

Raw Cane Sugars — Prewett's (as above).

Any brand of pure natural honey.

Molasses for use in place of treacle — Potter's (Herbal Supplies) Ltd, Leyland Mill Lane, Wigan, Lancs. WN1 2SB.

Rowse Molasses, and a wide selection of honey — Rowse Honey Ltd, Ewelme, Oxford.

Baked Products

Wholemeal pastry flan cases are available at: — Health food stores.

Biscuits — read labels carefully — Ethos Health Products, Nottington. Prewett's (as above).

Sweet Bars

Jordan's Original Crunchy Bar — coconut and honey (without almonds)

W. Jordan (Cereals) Ltd (as above).

Kalibu Carob Bar, also Carob Powder
Kalibu molasses bar

Holgram Foods Ltd, Granary House, Westmore Road, Burton-on-Trent, Staffordshire DE14 1TE.

Drinks

Pompadour Herb Teas

Tee Hendelsges, M.B.H. Düsseldorf, West Germany.

Barley Cup

Imported by Ridpath Pek Ltd, 1000 Newham Way, London E6 4JN.

Granose Swiss Cup

Granose Foods Ltd (as above).

Prewett's Chicory and Fruit Juices

Prewett's (as above).

Symingtons Dandelion Coffee

For full range of fruit and vegetable juices, tropical nectar and de-alcoholized wines write to:

G. R. Lane Health Products Ltd, Gloucester GL1 3QB.
Leisure Drinks Ltd, 16 The Green, Aston upon Trent, Derby DE7 2AA.

Water Filter

Easy and convenient to use, the Brita Water Filter is suitable for all drinking and cooking requirements, especially in heavily chlorinated or soft water areas. Heavy metal content is reduced i.e. lead, copper, etc. Lead in particular is virtually totally removed according to recent analyses. Filters out chlorine, scale chalk impurities etc. leaving pure water. Costs around £10.95. Replacement filters around £1.99. Treats approximately 80 litres of water. For stockists and further information write to Brita U.K. Ltd, 51 Ashley Road, Walton-on-Thames, Surrey KT12 1HG.

Toothpaste
Hollytrees Pure Lemon or Pure Fennel Toothpaste. Suitable for hyperactive and allergic people. Also for use with homoeopathic remedies. J. & D. Black Ltd., Holly Trees, 26 Hudson Road, Bexley Heath, Kent DA7 4PQ.

Deva Bridge Yogurt and Cheese Maker
No electricity needed. Deva Bridge Ltd, P.O. Box 5, Stowmarket, Suffolk, in health food shops or good hardware stores.

Cotton Clothing
For children and adults with problem skin, 100 per cent cotton clothing is best. For colour brochure please send stamp to: Cotton On, 29 North Clifton Street, Lytham FY8 5HW.

OTHER USEFUL ADDRESSES

Action Against Allergy, 43 The Downs, London SW20 8HG (s.a.e. please). Tel: 01-947-5082.

Asthma Society and Friends of the Asthma Research Council, 12 Pembridge Square, London W2 4EH. Tel: 01-229-1149.

Association for Breastfeeding Mothers, 131 Mayor Road, London SE26. Tel: 01-659-5151.

Clear (Campaign for Lead Free Air), 2 Northdown Street, London N1 9BG. Tel: 01-278 9686. Please enclose s.a.e.

The Coeliac Society, P.O. Box 181, London NW2 2QY.

Compassion in World Farming, 20 Lavant Street, Petersfield, Hampshire. Tel: Petersfield 64208.

The Farm and Food Society, 4 Willified Way, London NW11.

Foresight (Pre-Conceptual Care for Healthy Babies), Mrs Barnes, Woodhurst, Hydestile, Godalming, Surrey GU8 4AY. Tel: 04864 5743.

Henry Doubleday Research Association (National Organisation for Organic Gardeners), Convent Lane, Bocking, Braintree, Essex. Tel: 0376 24083.

Homoeopathic Medicine (an alternative to drugs). The Homoeopathic Development Foundation, Harcourt House, 19A Cavendish Square, London W1M 9AD. Tel: 01-629 3205.

Larkhall Allergy Testing Service (Cytotoxic and Food Antibody Tests), Larkhall Laboratories, 225 Putney Bridge Road, London SW15 2PY.

The McCarrison Society (Research into Good Nutrition), 23 Stanley Court, Worcester Road, Sutton, Surrey. Tel. 01-643 2812.

Milk Allergy Self Help Group, Secretary, Margaret Connock, 4 Queen Anne's Grove, Enfield, Middlesex EN1 2JP. Tel: 01-360 2348.

Ministry of Agriculture, Fisheries and Food, Great Westminster House, Horseferry Road, London SW1P 2AE. You can obtain a booklet of additives and their serial numbers from here.

National Anti-Fluoride Campaign, 36 Station Road, Thames Ditton, Surrey KT7 0NS. Tel: 01-398 2117.

The National Childbirth Trust, 9 Queensborough Terrace, London W2 3TB. Tel. 01-221 3833.

The National Eczema Society, Tavistock House North, Tavistock Square, London WC1H 9SR. Tel. 01-388 4097.

The National Play Bus Association, St. Thomas Church, St. Thomas Street, Bristol BS1. Tel: Bristol 0272 25951. Write to them to see if a play bus is available in your area.

National Society for Research into Allergy (N.S.R.A.), P.O. Box 45, Hinckley, Leicestershire LE10 1JY. S.A.E. please.

Opus — The National Co-ordinating Committee of OPUS is the umbrella name adopted by various groups — such as Parents Helpline, Parents Anonymous etc. which are operated by parents for parents under stress. For further information Tel: 0602 470551 Ext. 505.

Play Matters — The National Toy Libraries Association can be very helpful for a family with a hyperactive child who cannot cope with an ordinary playgroup. A book 'The Good Toy Guide', price £3.95, is available. For further information contact the Toy Libraries Association, Seabrook House, Darkes Lane, Potters Bar, Herts. EN6 2HL. Tel: 0707 44571.

Playgroup Places — The local County Council usually have a Playgroup Advisor. If you are having difficulties finding a place for your child these officers are usually most helpful.

Shaklee International, Central Milton Keynes MK9 2LS. Shaklee

Products include additive free nutritional supplements, personal care products and biogradable cleaners etc. Contact above address for local independent distributor.

The Society for Environmental Therapy, Andy Beckingham, Secretary, 3 Atherton Road, Ipswich, Suffolk IP2 9LD.

The Soil Association, Walnut Tree Manor, Haughley, Stowmarket, Suffolk IP14 3RS. Tel. 0449 673235.

Sports Facilities — Contact the Youth and Opportunities Officer at your District Council Offices. They should be able to help with details of facilities near you.

The Vegan Society, P.O. Box 3, Charlbury, Oxford OX7 6DU. Tel: 0993 831470.

The Vegetarian Society, 53 Marloes Road, Kensington, London W8 6LA. Tel: 01-937 7739.

York Medical and Nutritional Laboratories (Allergy, Cytotoxic Testing, for Food & Chemicals), 4 Museum Street, York YO1 2ES. Tel: 0904 52378.

APPENDIX IV

RECOMMENDED READING

Additives: Your Complete Survival Guide, Felicity Lawrence (Century)

Allergies — Your Hidden Enemy, Theron G. Randolph, M.D. (Thorsons Publishers Ltd)

Caring and Cooking for the Hyperactive Child, Mary Jane Finsand (Oak Tree Press Co. Ltd)

Chemical Victims (Masked Food and Chemical Allergies), Dr Richard Mackarness (Pan)

Diet, Crime and Delinquency, Alexander Schauss(Parker House, Berkeley, California)

Diet for a Small Planet (High Protein, Meatless Cooking), Frances Moore Lappe (Ballantine Books)

E for Additives, Maurice Hanssen (Thorsons Publishers Ltd)

Fast Food — Real Food, Miriam Polunin (Thorsons Publishers Ltd)

Feed Your Kids Right, Dr Lendon Smith (Delta)

Fluoridation and the Forgotten Issues, Dr Doris Grant (National Anti-Fluoridation Campaign, 36 Station Road, Thames Ditton, Surrey)

Food Additives, Eric Millstone (Penguin)

Good Food Gluten Free also *Good Food Grain Free* and *Milk Free* both by Hilda Cherry Hills (Roberts Publications)

Growing Up With Good Food (Allen & Unwin in association with the National Childbirth Trust)

Guide for Future Parents (Foresight Booklet), Mrs Barnes, Woodhurst, Hydestile, Godalming, Surrey

Guide to Natural Health, Constance Mellors (Granada)

Health Effects of Lead on Children (Conservation Society, 12A Guildhall Street, Chertsey, Surrey)

Learning Disabilities, Sylvia Farnham Diggory (Fontana)

Let's Eat Right To Keep Fit (Unwin); Let's Get Well (Unwin); Let's Have Healthy Children (Unwin) all by Adelle Davis

Living Dangerously, Hilda Cherry Hills (Roberts Publications)

Living with a Hyperactive Child, Miriam Wood (Souvenir Press)

Minerals — What They are and Why We Need Them, Miriam Polunin (Thorsons Publishers Ltd)

Natural Baby Foods, Anna Haycroft (Fontana)

Natural Foods Primer, B. Trum Hunter (Unwin)

Not All in the Mind (About Food Allergy), Dr Richard Mackarness (Pan)

Not Just a Load of Old Lentils (Vegetarian Cook Book), Rose Elliott (Fontana)

The Alternative Cookbook (Grain Free and Milk Free Recipes), Honor J. Campbell (Foodwatch, Butts Pond Industrial Estate, Sturminster Newton, Dorset DT10 1AZ)

The Allergy Problem, Dr V. Rippere (Thorsons Publishers Ltd)

The Foresight Wholefood Cookbook for Building Healthy Families, Norman and Ruth Jervis (Roberts Publications)

The Hyperactive Child, Belinda Barnes and Irene Colquhoun (Thorsons Publishers Ltd)

The Pulse Test (For Food Allergy), Dr A. Coca (Arco)

The Right Food For Your Kids, Louise Templeton (Century)

The Right Way to Eat, Miriam Polunin (Published by Dent in association with Ecoropa)

Why Your Child is Hyperactive, Dr Ben Feingold (Random House Press)

Vegetarian Mother and Baby Book, Rose Elliot (Fontana)

Zinc and Other Micro Nutrients, Dr C. Pfeiffer (Thorsons Publishers Ltd)

All the above books available from Wholefood, 24 Paddington Street, London W1. Tel: 01-935 3924.

A range of books dealing with allergy, emotional and behavioural problems are available from Merton Book Junkatique, 43 The Downs, London SW20. Please send s.a.e. for price list. This service is for members of Action Against Allergy (see page 263).

INDEX

Of further interest . . .

'E' FOR ADDITIVES

To meet growing consumer reaction against additives which may have an adverse effect on health, two major food chains have recently decided to stop using the most suspect 'E' additives in their own brand products. 'E' numbers represent the chemical additives used to process our food. From 1st January 1986, under EEC regulations, ALL pre-packaged foods will have to show their 'E' numbers in the list of ingredients. In some cases e.g. preservatives in meat, the additives safeguard our health, however the implications are that certain of them are non-essential — and perhaps even harmful — to sensitive people. Some of these chemicals cause migraine, hyperactivity, nausea, severe abdominal pain or even more serious conditions. 'E' FOR ADDITIVES by **Maurice Hanssen** is a clearly presented guide to the uses and possible side-effects of chemical additives. A MUST *for people who care about what they eat.*